T0399001

Outsourcing Duty

Outsourcing Duty

The Moral Exploitation of the American Soldier

MICHAEL J. ROBILLARD AND
BRADLEY J. STRAWSER

OXFORD
UNIVERSITY PRESS

OXFORD
UNIVERSITY PRESS

Oxford University Press is a department of the University of Oxford. It furthers
the University's objective of excellence in research, scholarship, and education
by publishing worldwide. Oxford is a registered trade mark of Oxford University
Press in the UK and certain other countries.

Published in the United States of America by Oxford University Press
198 Madison Avenue, New York, NY 10016, United States of America.

© Oxford University Press 2022

All rights reserved. No part of this publication may be reproduced, stored in
a retrieval system, or transmitted, in any form or by any means, without the
prior permission in writing of Oxford University Press, or as expressly permitted
by law, by license, or under terms agreed with the appropriate reproduction
rights organization. Inquiries concerning reproduction outside the scope of the
above should be sent to the Rights Department, Oxford University Press, at the
address above.

You must not circulate this work in any other form
and you must impose this same condition on any acquirer.

Library of Congress Cataloging-in-Publication Data
Names: Robillard, Michael, author. | Strawser, Bradley Jay, author.
Title: Outsourcing duty : the moral exploitation of the American soldier /
Michael J. Robillard, Bradley J. Strawser.
Other titles: Moral exploitation of the American soldier
Description: New York, NY : Oxford University Press, [2022] |
Includes bibliographical references and index. | Contents: Foreword /
by Nancy Sherman—Exploitiation vs. moral exploitation—The moral
exploitation of soldiers—Soldier, citizen, and state—Connections—
Prescriptions—Conclusion—Epilogue / by Cheyney Ryan—
Appendix: Criticisms, questions, & responses.
Identifiers: LCCN 2021051854 | ISBN 9780190671457 (hardback) |
ISBN 9780190671488 (oso) | ISBN 9780190671471 (epub) | ISBN 9780190671464 (pdf)
Subjects: LCSH: Military service, Voluntary—United States—Moral and
ethical aspects. | Civil-military relations—United States. |
Exploitation.
Classification: LCC UB323 .R63 2021 | DDC 355.2/230973—dc23/eng/20211115
LC record available at https://lccn.loc.gov/2021051854

DOI: 10.1093/oso/9780190671457.001.0001

1 3 5 7 9 8 6 4 2

Printed by Sheridan Books, Inc., United States of America

Dedicated to my father, Daniel, and my mother, Denise
I owe you everything
—Michael

Dedicated to my children, Toby and Norah
You are my light
—Bradley

We also dedicate this book to the memory of our friend, colleague,
brother, and comrade at arms, Major Ian Fishback, PhD. Ian's
untimely passing in many ways tragically exemplifies the point of
this book: the inverted priorities of our contemporary American
society, and yet another heartbreaking consequence of our nation's
continued civic neglect with respect to the wars that it fights and the
warriors it sends to fight them. Ian was a man of principle and an
incredible example of moral courage both from within the ranks and
from without. We pray that he rest in peace and that his death not be
in vain.

War must be, while we defend our lives against a destroyer who would devour all; but I do not love the bright sword for its sharpness, nor the arrow for its swiftness, nor the warrior for his glory. I love only that which they defend.

—J.R.R. Tolkien

Contents

Foreword

Soldiers, though they fight in cadres to serve country and causes larger than themselves, typically think of their resilience as a matter of personal strength and grit. "Embrace the suck," while an inelegant phrase, captures the mindset for many. Be a stoic warrior. And if you're not, it's a personal failing, or maybe a sign that you're not cut out for the warrior culture. All the horrors of war, the psychological, physical, and moral challenges are tests of *you*, your courage, your honor, your luck. Injury—physical, psychological, and moral—are yours. And healing and repair are also yours. They define a veteran's life of coming home and reintegrating.

But what if the burdens you bear are unfairly or disproportionately placed upon you by a civilian public? What if you are morally exploited as a vulnerable group? What if a country's duty is "outsourced" on a vulnerable 1% of the population who, as a result, take on disproportionate moral burdens endemic to war? If that's the case, then the conversation shifts from character and the moral psychology of warrior resilience to systemic injustice and institutional conditions that create profoundly unfair moral burdening on those who go to war.

This is the focus of Michael Robillard and B. J. Strawser's fine book. Both are graduates of military academies, both teach or have taught military officers, both have spent most of their professional careers immersed in military culture, both come from military families. Michael is an Iraq War veteran and an Army Ranger. They are insiders. They are insiders who argue that many who sign up to serve at seventeen or eighteen as they did, or earlier, as B. J. did, were "recruited in some sense for nearly my entire life as part of a military family." And yet they also argue that they are not victims to be pitied. They are writing not to muster pity, but to right a deep structural injustice that is the fallout of the current all-volunteer army.

Their concerns may sound familiar and voiced often since the end of the Vietnam era conscription. An all-volunteer force draws from a vulnerable demographic—easily exploitable in virtue of socioeconomic class, geographic location, age, gender, family background, and more. The promise of a subsidized education, the chance to travel and see the world, the possibility of better employment after, the chance to serve and be patriotic and prove your mettle against a worthy adversary are incentives for many to sign up. But they are also incentives easily preyed upon by recruiters and recruiting material that misrepresent the real costs and burdens of warfighting. Recruiters recruit adolescents, younger than those who in this country can legally purchase alcohol. And yet those who are being recruited for military service will be required to take on much more responsibility than many underage drinkers. Many will have to make split-second decisions in population-centric warfare, negotiate with corrupt warlords, walk troops through terrain riddled with mines and improvised explosive devices. Does recruitment really take into account the neurological, epistemic, and cognitive limitations that come with adolescence? Quotas likely couldn't be reached if they did. But that means one small sliver of the population makes the sacrifices for all. They may do so willingly, as part of the lofty call to duty, honor, or country. But taking on the moral risks and responsibilities of military service on behalf of others leaves them unfairly burdened not just in the act of signing up but also in "ongoing morally exploitative relationships." And this is especially so in an era when troops are forced to deploy multiple times in endless wars.

The military sociologist Charles Moskos argued decades ago that an all-volunteer force makes far too little demand on most of American citizenry. He urged a return to conscription as one tier of three within a system of mandatory national youth service. This is how we share civic responsibility and civic duty, he argued. Military conscription would not exempt those at the top of the social ladder. Needless to say, the argument was a political non-starter. While Robillard and Strawser outline at the end of the book policy options, one of which is dubbed "skin in the game" (i.e., mandatory conscription), policy is not their primary focus. What they are interested in is conceptual analysis: The moral exploitation of soldiers as a result of structural and institutional factors and the downstream effects of that exploitation.

The downstream effects are what I know best from my work with service members and veterans over many decades. Too few who are too young and too vulnerable shoulder too much moral responsibility. The result is often profound moral injury—a sense of shattered moral identity, sometimes to do with their own transgressions, real or apparent; other times to do with profound wrongs suffered at the hands of commanders who betray them or violate their trusts; still others to do with what they witness up close. Moral injury and its emotions—guilt and shame, resentment and rage, can rack a soul for a lifetime. Moral repair, through self-empathy, forgiveness, therapy, and service are all ways soldiers try to come home.[1]

This is to focus on the individual—what feels like to be overburdened with moral responsibility in a high-stakes situation and to live with the moral anguish of decisions you wish you hadn't made that take a buddy's life, or that kill a young child in a collateral incident under permissive rules of engagement. The examples are too many in war. Take Lalo Panyagua who gave permission to one of his fellow marines, Corporal Justin Wilson, to leave the MRAP to relieve himself, only to be blown up by an improvised

[1] See N. Sherman, *Stoic Warriors: The Ancient Philosophy behind the Military Mind* (Oxford, 2005); idem, *The Untold War: Inside the Hearts, Minds, and Souls of Our Soldiers* (New York, 2010); idem, *Afterwar: Healing the Moral Injuries of our Soldiers* (Oxford , 2015); *Stoic Wisdom: Ancient Lessons for Modern Resilience* (Oxford, 2021).

explosive device. For years, Lalo was haunted with what he could have and should have done: "I could have said through the radio to the squad, 'Don't forget to reinforce the area.'" Once he got injured, "I could have pushed harder" to get the sergeant on site to call in medevac faster. "I'm the guy in charge," he repeated to me over and over. "They're my kids." And I didn't take care of "my baby birds." This is the personal moral profile, here to do with a young nineteen-year-old in charge of a squad fighting in a mine-ridden area near the Helmand River in Afghanistan. He joined the Corps on the cusp of eighteen as a way to leave the LA barrio, to serve nobly, and belong to a cause larger than himself and more honorable than a street gang.[2]

Or take CDR Layne McDowell, a Naval Academy graduate and F/A-18 pilot whose memory of flying sorties over Kosovo in an F-14 squadron haunt him. It was a midday strike on a radio-relay site in northern Kosovo May 1999. Intelligence imagery was grainy. In order not to alert Serbian forces, he had to go south of the target and make a quick turn back. Aircrews now had less time to locate and verify the target. Serbian Air Defense opened up fire and that took McDowell's attention away from the targeting screen. "I felt good about the release. Then clouds obscured the target until about 13 seconds to impact. At that time I began having doubts about the target. It didn't look right, but in those 13 seconds, I didn't say anything, and we took out what we were targeting with 2 GBU [guided bomb unit]-12's."

Dread started to mount. Back on the carrier, McDowell looked at the strike footage on a big screen. The bomb had struck not the target but a carport next to a house. McDowell saw signs of civilian occupation, and unmistakably, four bikes, two of which were child-sized.

There were never any legal proceedings or Navy follow-up to determine if and who and how many civilians and children may have

---

[2] See Sherman, *Afterwar,* 57–74, 150–52.

been killed in the strike. But he carries the moral burden in a repetitive, intrusive dream in which he conducts his own after-incident investigation. The dream replayed again just before he was deployed to Iraq in 2005 and was not far from his thoughts in his air war in Afghanistan. In the dream, the building he bombed was somehow still standing but there was thick dust everywhere, insulation and wires dangling, boards littered all over the ground. The smoke was thick, and it was hard to make out who, at all, was in the structure. He aches to turn back the clock, to be given time to steer the bomb to an empty field. But he can't. In the structure, he definitely saw a small boy huddled in the corner, coated in dust, severely injured but still breathing. He knew the face. It was McDowell's own son, Landon. "He lifted the boy to his chest, tightly for a hug, cupping his hand behind the child's little head, to hold it. The back of his skull was gone."[3]

These are examples of moral injury. But Robillard and Strawser focus not on the individual narrative and arc of moral injury. Their implicit claim is that listening to the voices of war is not a sufficient way of sharing the public burden. It goes beyond the thin crust of "thank you for your service," but it doesn't address the underlying *social* ill. It doesn't expose the inequity in our public system of collective warfighting. Too few—only 1% of the population—whether they are enlisted or officers—bear the "increased moral deliberative roles, increased exposure to moral risk, and increased likelihood of incurring moral residue, or 'dirty hands,' that come with warfighting." The argument of this book is that that segment of the population is being morally exploited.

---

[3] I have drawn this case from American journalist C. J. Chivers's *The Fighters* (Simon & Schuster, 2018), 6–24, 119–121. I am grateful for correspondence and conversation with Chris Chivers about this account. See also Chivers's story about McDowell and changes in the rules of engagement in air war from Kosovo to Afghanistan in C.J. Chivers, "A Changed Way of War in Afghanistan's Skies," *New York Times*, January 15, 2012, https://www.nytimes.com/2012/01/16/world/asia/afghan-war-reflects-changes-in-air-war.html

The idea of wrongful exploitation is familiar. It typically involves taking unfair advantage of another's vulnerable position—maybe an immigrant worker, without reasonable options for employment, consenting to work in a meatpacking plant where the risks and dangers of the working conditions, especially in the tine of a pandemic, may outweigh the benefits for the worker.[4] The exploitation involves an unfair exchange of tangible goods or services. The centerpiece of Robillard and Strawser's argument is that there is another distinct species of exploitation "that involves unfairly burdening someone with added moral responsibility or moral decision-making." The burden is moral, in a very literal sense: Soldiers shoulder in a profound and unfair way the *inner moral weight* of making decisions about going to war and fighting in war. That moral load is carried by many who are still under the legal drinking age and, until recently, under the voting age. Current just war theory debates about the individual moral responsibility of soldiers, and whether just conduct in war is ever separable from cause, are far from abstract once seen through the lens of too few and too vulnerable a segment of the population shouldering too much tough moral deliberation in the name of public service.

In short, *Outsourcing Duty* is a much-needed book. It exposes an ugly form of exploitation that we have ignored for far too long. It is a call to arms to share and distribute the cost of the public good of defense more fairly. It is a call to a kind of "justice as fairness."[5]

Nancy Sherman
Georgetown University

[4] For a penetrating expose of exploitation in the Smithfield pork factory, listen to this episode of the "The Daily," https://www.nytimes.com/2020/05/04/podcasts/the-daily/meat-processing-coronavirus.html

[5] J. Rawls, *Theory of Justice* (Cambridge, MA, 1971), 3 though Rawls himself often demurred from applications of his theory of justice.

Acknowledgments

We would like to thank and acknowledge the following people and institutions who were pivotal in this book's realization (in no particular order): Hallie Liberto, Paul Bloomfield, Suzy Killmister, Michael Lynch, Daniel Silvermint, Don Baxter, the University of Connecticut Philosophy Department, the Stockdale Center for Ethical Leadership, the United States Naval Academy, the Naval Postgraduate School, John Arquilla, David Alderson, Kalev Sepp, Tristan Volpe, Siamak Naficy, Doug Borer, Naval Special Warfare, Brad Voigt, Abbi Strawser, Ed Barrett, Daniel Halliday, Tony Coady, the University of Melbourne, Cheyney Ryan, Nancy Sherman, David Luban, Jeff McMahan, Guy Sela, Cecile Fabre, Helen Frowe, Jonathan Parry, Lars Christie, Thomas Simpson, Yitzhak Benbaji, Victor Tadros, Marissa Kemp, Jonathan Moreno, MAJ Nicholas Utzig, LTC Bob Underwood, LTC Bill Nance, Knute L. Amrisk, MAJ Scott Orr, LTC Jon Huntsman, COL Mike Richardson, Andrew Bacevich, SOCS Rico Madaffari, Barry Lam, Lisa Strutz, Aderogba Ayoola, Margaret McGreevy, Mia Lecinski, Seumas Miller, Julian Savulescu, the Uehiro Center for Practical Ethics, the University of Oxford, the Ethics, Law, and Armed Conflict Center, the European Research Council Advanced Grant on Global Terrorism and Collective Moral Responsibility, the Notre Dame Technology Ethics Center, and the Notre Dame Institute for Advanced Studies.

Additionally, our heartfelt appreciation and gratitude to Oxford University Press, especially Peter Ohlin and his team for their continued support throughout this book's long journey.

Introduction

Theirs not to reason why,
Theirs but to do and die

—*Alfred Lord Tennyson,*
Charge of the Light Brigade

Let us begin with a story about a man we'll call Tom. We've changed
his name, but this is a true story. Tom is a major in the US Army.
He's served on active duty now for about a decade, deployed once to
Iraq and twice to Afghanistan in that time. He's presently stationed
at Fort Bragg in North Carolina as an Army Special Forces Officer—
formerly known as a "Green Beret." In his daily life, Tom notices
some trends in the relationship society at large seems to have toward him as a soldier.[1] For example, when Tom goes to the movies,
he gets a discounted ticket. The movies being played at the theater
regularly include at least one or two films that glorify military service—often, he knows now, unrealistically. On his drive to go watch
a movie, he sees a minivan with the ubiquitous big yellow magnetic
ribbon affixed to the back. Under it are the words "We Support
the Troops" emblazoned for all to see. He's unsure if these things
are heartfelt or simply a kind of modern-day virtue signaling—or

---

[1] For the purposes of this book, we will use the common term "soldier" interchange-
ably as a generic reference to all American soldiers, sailors, veterans, and members of the
armed service.

Outsourcing Duty. Michael J. Robillard and Bradley J. Strawser, Oxford University Press. © Oxford
University Press 2022. DOI: 10.1093/oso/9780190671457.003.0001

perhaps both. When he's at a sporting event that weekend—a college football game with all its pageantry—he watches a kind of morality play acted out at halftime. A soldier, it seems, is home from war. It comes to a head for Tom when, after this display, the announcer asks all military servicemembers and veterans to please stand as the rest of the stadium praises them with thunderous applause. To Tom, it all feels a bit garish.

While this is all happening, Tom reflects on how he first decided to join the military. He knows far more now than he could have ever known then about what it is like to actually serve in the military and to go to war—and what comes with it.

A woman seated next to Tom, noticing his short haircut, his clean-shaven face, and his general awkwardness during this moment turns to him and asks,

"Are you in the military?"

"Yes," Tom replies.

"Thank you for your service," she says back to him.

He then responds in exasperation, "Please don't thank me. I'm sorry. It doesn't feel right."

The woman, perhaps understandably, is confused and a bit taken aback. She simply wanted to thank Tom for his service. But what she doesn't understand, and what Tom only partially grasps himself, is the disconnect, the gaping chasm between her sentimental words and the reality of his lived experience as a soldier and as an instrument of American foreign policy.

These phrases that Tom recoils from have become common parlance within mainstream American discourse. Yet despite the omnipresence of these pithy slogans and bumper-sticker sayings, despite the yellow ribbons and the parades, the dedicated fitness workouts and sporting event recognition days, despite the video games, Hollywood blockbusters, and bestselling books, despite the seeming overabundance of recognition and near constant surplus of praise for "the troops" within contemporary civilian society, something is nonetheless amiss. Something is very wrong.

Indeed, throughout most American college campuses in this country, many students, if randomly asked, could likely provide sophisticated arguments and highly nuanced viewpoints pertaining to their individual moral relationship to issues such as vegetarianism, animal welfare, climate change, social justice, class, race, and gender. However, when asked about their thoughts on their relationship to America's soldiers and to the wars America presently fights on their behalf, students' answers are usually lacking in similar sophistication and complexity, to wildly understate the matter—or often lacking even a recognition of the moral issue itself. Indeed, a similar degree of disengagement, social malaise, and complicity can likewise be noticed beyond college campuses within the public at large. What's more, the average American, if randomly surveyed, could likely more easily name five new reality television stars, pop music icons, or celebrity chefs over the last twelve months than they could name five war heroes, who fought on their behalf, over the past two decades let alone a singular name of a deceased veteran within their own local voting precinct. Meanwhile, Hollywood actors receive millions of dollars and social acclaim for pretending to be soldiers on the big screen and faux service member dog tags are worn as chic accessories on Paris fashion runways.

Despite such social detachment, frequent cartoonish caricatures of the American soldier as either lionized hero beyond reproach or as pitiable victim worthy of infinite sympathy abound across the media and are regular tropes within the 24-hour news cycle and, consequently, in the public consciousness. Such caricatures, however, often do more to stymy and hinder the capacity for authentic, nuanced, and sometimes difficult discussion and debate concerning civilian society's relationship to soldiers, to American foreign policy, and to war itself. What's more, such caricatures and aforementioned slogans often serve to paper over and sanitize a much more pernicious state of social and institutional affairs and betray a level of public disengagement and chance for open and honest dialogue and reflection.

Accordingly, one way of understanding our aim in this book is to take the reported moral experiences of modern American soldiers more seriously. Anyone reading this has no doubt long heard stories of various problems plaguing the contemporary American veteran community, problems like PTSD, societal isolation, suicide, divorce, unemployment, homelessness, and general trouble reintegrating into civilian life. But here's another: *Many military members describe feeling as if they are bearing some particular kind of duty or moral responsibility that the majority of society seems to have shirked.* This is not the obvious point that military members have chosen to "serve," as our contemporary locution tends to describe it, while civilians have not. Rather, it's a perceived sense of an almost willful ignorance and lack of concern from the rest of society over military matters, foreign policy, and the moral realities of those wars we ask soldiers to fight on our behalf. And, soldiers tell us, this disjunction is not only frustrating but also comes across as something deeply unfair or, even, unjust.

Political theorist and Vietnam veteran, Andrew Bacevich, famously describes this feeling as a "breach of trust" between the society that sends its military to war and those military members themselves. Bacevich writes:

> *From pulpit and podium, at concerts and sporting events, expressions of warmth and affection shower down on the troops. Yet when those wielding power in Washington subject soldiers to serial abuse, Americans acquiesce. When the state heedlessly and callously exploits those same troops, the people avert their gaze. Maintaining a pretence for caring about soldiers, state, and society actually collaborate in betraying them.*[2]

[2] Andrew Bacevich, *Breach of Trust: How Americans Failed Their Soldiers and Their Country* (New York, 2013).

In some capacity or other, we have taught, worked with, mentored, loved, and been in regular contact with military members across many countries over the past twenty-plus years apiece, forty years in total. In our combined time teaching ethics at the Naval Postgraduate School, the US Air Force Academy, the US Naval Academy, Naval Special Warfare, and the greater US military community, we often find ourselves in gut-wrenching conversations over a soldier's relationship to the society he or she serves. At times, we often end up hearing military members express some variant of the following series of questions.

"Do you think the shoe salesman or banker or bartender down the street from here has any real sense of military issues or the things that we soldiers do?"

"Do your average fellow citizens even know that we are (still) at war?"

"Do most people have any kind of daily awareness of what those who fight on their behalf are doing?. . . Or that there even are people fighting on their behalf?"

And so on. These conversations are disquieting. And the responses the soldiers give to these nearly rhetorical questions are strong, consistent, and depressing—because the answers are uniformly and unequivocally a firm "no." Tragically, the best survey data we have of the general population of the United States confirms these views as accurate. Americans are notoriously uninformed about matters large and small—we are awash in general ignorance. But Americans' ignorance of foreign policy and military affairs perhaps tops them all. Finally, undergirding these discussions and frustrations are the self-reported feelings that result from this disconnect: An often hard to articulate, but very much real, sense of an unequal distribution of societal and civic duty. Something is "off" in the grand equation of justice and fairness.

Given such firsthand lived experiences and accounts, what we aim to do in this book is to take seriously this feeling of disproportionate moral concern or shouldering of moral duty that soldiers so often report. Then, we aim to give this reported experience a thorough philosophical moral analysis and, hopefully, a better explanation and understanding of it. Just what, exactly, is going on when so many modern-day soldiers feel so alienated from the very population they purportedly serve? What is the moral failing or injustice occurring when a society as a whole divorces itself from its civic duty to engage in matters of war and peace? Is this even a moral failing at all? What is the shared moral burden that should fall upon the shoulders of the everyday man or woman? And, whatever that is, can a society be derelict in that duty? If it can be—and we will argue that contemporary society is indeed derelict in this particular duty— then how does that affect the soldiers who do in fact shoulder the moral burdens of war on behalf of us all? We will not only give a robust explanation of this moral reality and some of the underlying causes behind it, but we will also explore some potential ways it could be mitigated.

To go a bit deeper: There appears to be a real sense in which the moral burdens of contemporary war are oftentimes unfairly outsourced to soldiers alone, when, as a moral fact, the society that sends, commands, and employs those soldiers properly holds a large share of that very same responsibility. It is this unfair outsourcing of moral responsibility, from society at large to its professional soldiers, that we believe is at the core of the morally troubling treatment of soldiers. In our analysis of this phenomenon, we believe that its unique unfairness can best be explained and articulated through the language of exploitation.[3]

---

[3] See Michael Robillard and Bradley Strawser, "The Moral Exploitation of Soldiers," *Public Affairs Quarterly*, 30 (2016). In this section we rely heavily on some of our claims and language made in that article.

Wrongful exploitation is generally conceived of as taking unfair advantage of or garnering excessive benefit from another's vulnerability. In such cases, the exploiter makes use of the exploitee's vulnerability and absence of reasonable options to gain benefits, often with the exploitee's consent that would otherwise not be granted. Contemporary theories of exploitation have largely formulated this unfair transaction in terms of an exchange involving some sort of tangible, material good or service. This, however, is not always the case.

In this book we advance two main ideas. First, with regard to a theory of wrongful exploitation in general, we contend that in addition to instances of exploitation involving the unfair exchange of physical goods or services, there exists a unique *species* of exploitation that involves unfairly burdening someone with added moral responsibility or moral decision-making. We call this special type of exploitation "*moral exploitation.*" Second, we contend that (at least some) contemporary soldiers are unfairly burdened in this way as part of their military service and resulting forced moral choices made in and about war. That is, the plight of many modern soldiers provides a paradigm case of moral exploitation worth exploring to better understand this distinct phenomenon. It is also worth exploring in its own right. For if it is true that soldiers are being morally exploited, this has implications for the present debate within just war theory regarding, among other things, the doctrine of the moral equality of combatants and what its rejection entails for the individual moral responsibility of soldiers. This concept likewise helps us better understand the notion of "moral injury" and its acute prevalence in communities of returning war veterans.

Moral injury refers to a psychological harm resulting from transgressing one's own moral code or from committing some kind of wrong. Given the profound set of moral ambiguities inherent both in war and in a state's act of going to war, one can quickly see how exposed soldiers are to situations where incidents of moral injury are likely, if not inevitable. While it is understood that part of the burden of being a soldier is the acceptance of the possibility, if not high likelihood, of physical danger, as well as physical and psychological hardship, the extent of the burden that the common soldier accepts fails to be exhausted by the domain of the physical. Rather, in addition to the array of physical and psychological burdens that a soldier is expected to take on, there is also a set of profound and weighty moral burdens that the agent is expected to shoulder once he or she consents to join the profession of arms. If, however, the agent's initial consent was fundamentally derived from his or her pronounced vulnerability (be it socioeconomic, cognitive, age related, or otherwise), then it would seem that the recruit or would-be soldier could not have reasonably refused to transact with the military body in the first place, in at least some cases. And in that scenario, therefore, he or she could not have refused the additional moral responsibility and potential blameworthiness thrust upon him or her. The consequences of such a relationship, then, is that the likelihood of incurring what are known as morally "dirty hands" becomes yet another burden that the most vulnerable and disenfranchised of society must bear.

Moreover, the extent of moral responsibility placed on soldiers is something many are not fully aware of when they join the military, particularly if we include the moral burden of deciding whether to even go to war. The result of such a transaction, in effect, is a sort of off-loading of moral responsibility and blameworthiness from society to a very small minority of often vulnerable agents. If true, this understanding of the moral exploitation of soldiers could have significant implications within contemporary just war theory and our understanding of how we should properly adjudicate individual responsibility and liability in war.

The structure of this book will proceed as follows. In Chapter 1, we consider various competing theories of exploitation and investigate the unique wrongness of exploitation. In that chapter we also introduce and unpack our concept of what we have called moral exploitation. This concept involves cases whereby individuals or groups are exploited by being unfairly overloaded with moral responsibility, moral risk, or overexposure to "dirty hands" scenarios. In Chapter 2, we explore how the concept and phenomena of moral exploitation applies specifically to the modern-day American soldier and recruit. More specifically, we look at the ways soldiers are historically vulnerable to regular exploitation within society and how such vulnerability also makes them vulnerable to the outsourcing or piling on of additional moral responsibility, moral risk, and instances of dirty hands. In Chapter 3, we explore several metaphysical and normative conceptions of the state and how these different conceptions affect our notion of shared duties between soldiers and citizens. In Chapter 4, we consider some broader philosophical and societal connections related to this issue of moral exploitation and the outsourcing of moral responsibility. And in Chapter 5, taking the moral exploitation of soldiers seriously, we offer several prescriptions, both ex ante and ex post, and offer recommendations as to how the state, the military institution, and American society at large can and ought to respond to this phenomenon. Lastly, in the Appendix, we consider several major counterarguments, questions, and objections related to this concept of moral exploitation generally, as well as to the moral exploitation of soldiers more specifically.

Before we proceed further, however, we must first make a disclaimer and address what we will refer to here as the *Veteran's Paradox*. The Veteran's Paradox can be summarized as follows: As a veteran, how can one voice opinions on the military and its policies without falling prey to the binary of sounding either like a pacifistic victim or a war-hawk shill? If one veers too close to the former, then one runs the risk of sounding like a broken victim or making soldiers out to be broken victims *or* sounding like a person condemning one's own country, military, and comrades at arms. If one veers too close to the latter, then one runs the risk of conflating patriotism with enthusiastic, uncritical endorsement of all things military and all things war. As a result, the instinct within veterans to assertively stick up for one's self or for one's military brothers and sisters or, conversely, to voice measured and thoughtful criticism of existing military foreign policy or institutional schemes, often becomes mentally short-circuited before such ideas can find full and proper expression. A tightrope must therefore be walked between these common narrative lanes of victim and war hawk if one hopes to say anything new or insightful. That being said, this book will be our attempt to walk that very tightrope. Let us then be clear that within these pages we do not claim to speak on behalf of every soldier, or every veteran, or anyone beyond just ourselves for that matter. Furthermore, let us also be clear that this book should not be mistaken or misunderstood as a case of special pleading or a demand for pity or an instance of two veterans jockeying for a better position on the present-day victimhood hierarchy. Rather, it is, at the very least, a call for dialogue, albeit, a *better* dialogue, between America and its troops and between America and itself, where war and the experiences of soldiers are taken more seriously. This is not to say that many civilians are not earnest and sincere in their commitments and concerns regarding soldiers. Certainly, many are, of course. However, our aim is simply to put better and more precise language on a yet to be well-articulated feeling that many Americans, both soldiers and civilians alike, have been sensing for some time now. We hope to do so in such a way that the refrigerator hum of the "forever war" may be heard more loudly within the forefront of the American social imagination, and, from behind that hum, the voices, experiences, and spirit of the *other* 1%.

1

Exploitation versus
Moral Exploitation

He thought he'd 'list, perhaps,
Off-hand like—just as I—
Was out of work—had sold his traps—
No other reason why.

—Thomas Hardy, *The Man He Killed*[1]

Introduction

Exploitation is often defined as garnering unfair or excessive benefit by taking advantage of another person's or group's vulnerability. When people hear the word "exploitation" they typically
think of macro-level social phenomena like sweatshop labor, child
labor, organ sales, and prostitution or micro-level phenomena
like exploitative personal relationships or discrete transactions on
the free market. And while many scholars have recognized that
there is a substantive moral distinction between *exploiting a situation* and *exploiting a person*, as Robert Goodin notes, it is this
latter normatively laden understanding of exploitation with which
contemporary ethicists are primarily focused.[2] It is this type of

[1] Thomas Hardy, "The Man He Killed," *Harper's Weekly*, November 8, 1902. By "list"
the author here means the act of "enlisting" in the military; a common vernacular usage
at the time.
[2] Robert Goodin, *Exploiting a Situation and Exploiting a Person* (University of
Essex, 1985).

Outsourcing Duty. Michael J. Robillard and Bradley J. Strawser, Oxford University Press. © Oxford
University Press 2022. DOI: 10.1093/oso/9780190671457.003.0002

person-centered exploitation we wish to explore in this opening chapter. By first laying the careful philosophical groundwork of exploitation in general, as well as explicating a distinct species of exploitation that we call "moral exploitation," we can then explore in subsequent chapters how this form of exploitation is often instantiated in cases involving modern soldiers.

Starting Definitions

Theorists often formulate exploitation in two distinct ways. One way formulates exploitation in terms of an unfair *transfer* of some kind of good, service, or commodity in the free market.[3] Alternatively, exploitation is also sometimes formulated as some kind of ongoing unfair *relationship* of varying scale, such as the relationship between two romantic partners, between colleges and student-athletes, or between capital and labor. We'll call one transactional exploitation and the other relational exploitation. These two different general ways of approaching exploitation will be a critically helpful distinction for the majority of our work in this book. We will return to this key distinction later in the chapter. First, however, allow us to explain exploitation of all kinds more generally as a kind of wrongful or unjust distribution resulting from disparate vulnerabilities or positioning between groups and actors.

This general theme, of an unfair or lopsided distribution of an emergent surplus generated from a transactional exchange or structural relationship, can be seen in many traditional as well as contemporary definitions of exploitation. Consider some of the following definitions offered by scholars who work on exploitation. Barrington Moore, in some of the earliest work on exploitation

---

[3] As a note to the reader, we borrow much of the structural parsing of the core concepts surrounding exploitation from Matt Zwolinski's excellent *Stanford Encyclopedia of Philosophy* article "Exploitation" located at https://plato.stanford.edu/entries/exploitation/.

in contemporary analytic philosophy, defines exploitation this way: Exploitation forms part of an exchange of goods and services when (1) the goods and services exchanged are quite obviously not of equivalent value, and (2) one party to the exchange uses a substantial degree of coercion.[4] While Mikhail Valdman, one of the more prolific recent philosophers to work on exploitation, puts it this way:

> To wrongly exploit someone is to extract excessive benefits from him—it is to use the fact that his back is to the wall, so to speak, to get him to accept lopsided and outrageous terms of exchange.

Valdman goes on to stress that

> one wrongly exploits another if and only if one extracts excessive benefits from someone who cannot, or cannot reasonably, refuse one's offer.[5]

Hallie Liberto, another prominent scholar writing on exploitation, sums up the recent state of affairs where most contemporary philosophers come down on how to define exploitation:

> Exploitation theorists usually stipulate two necessary and jointly sufficient conditions for an act being one of wrongful exploitation. There must be something morally problematic about the gain that the exploiter achieves (e.g. the gain is unfair or is motivated by opportunism). One might call this the "Advantage Clause." In addition, there is some predicament that must characterize the

---

[4] Barrington Moore, *Reflections on the Causes of Human Misery* (Boston, 1973), 53, quoted in Alan Wertheimer, *Exploitation* (New Jersey, 1996), 12. As we'll discuss later, the consensus on whether coercion must be present to instantiate exploitation has shifted.

[5] Mikhail Valdman, "A Theory of Wrongful Exploitation," *Philosophers' Imprint*, 9 (2009), 1–14, 10.

circumstances of the exploited   persons (e.g. a condition of desperation or a state of being without options). I will call this the "Vulnerability Clause."[6]

Of course, for many, the very concept of exploitation also has deeper roots in broader societal structures. Some key thinkers, both historically and more recently, have argued that this includes, most notably, entire economic-political states of affairs (such as capitalism) that have exploitative relationships or transactional arrangements at their core. Jeffrey Reiman, for example, argues:

> A society is exploitative, when its social structure is organized so that unpaid labor is systematically forced out of one class and put at the disposal of another.... Any exploitative society is a form of slavery.[7]

While Nancy Holmstrom goes further:

> It is the fact that the capitalist's income is derived through forced, unpaid, surplus wage labor, the product of which the workers do not control, that makes wage labor exploitative.[8]

Or, most famously of all, Karl Marx took this understanding of exploitation to be endemic and intrinsic to modern economics. Marx understood exploitation to be the standard relationship for most workers by virtue of having to sell their labor to capitalists, but for resultingly less compensation value than their labor actually produces.

---

[6] Hallie Liberto, "Exploitation and the Vulnerability Clause," *Ethical Theory and Moral Practice*, 17, no. 4 (2014), 619.

[7] J. Reiman, "Exploitation, Force, and the Moral Assessment of Capitalism: Thoughts on Roemer and Cohen," *Philosophy and Public Affairs*, 16 (1987), 3–41.

[8] Nancy Holmstrom, "Exploitation," *Canadian Journal of Philosophy* 7, no 2 (1977) 353–369.

The bourgeoisie . . . has resolved personal worth into exchange value, and in place of the numberless indefeasible chartered freedoms, has set up that single, unconscionable freedom—Free Trade. In one word, for exploitation, veiled by religious and political illusions, it has substituted naked, shameless, direct, brutal exploitation.[9]

Nearly all of these understandings of exploitation, from the interpersonal to the societal-economic-political, involve a key notion of acceptable and unacceptable costs being traded in an unfair or disproportionate manner. However, many scholars, such as Valdman, have noted that even with the general idea of exploitation understood as a rough concept, "it is difficult to give a precise account of when one's non-transaction costs are unacceptable."[10] Valdman goes on, however, to cite Stuart White's framing of the concept in terms of market vulnerability: "C's urgent need for some good and D's monopoly over that good permits D to wrongfully exploit C."[11] While not quite giving us the clarity we still need for acceptable versus unacceptable costs and transactions, White's framing here is a helpful starting point for our exploration of exploitation.

Conceptual Distinctness of Exploitation

Generally speaking, philosophers regard cases of exploitation as being conceptually distinct from cases of coercion in that in cases of coercion, the coercee's overall set of reasonable options often decreases in virtue of some kind of threat or restriction, whereas in cases of exploitation, the exploitee's overall set of options actually

---

[9] Karl Marx, *The Communist Manifesto* (Pacifica, CA, 1848), 30, https://www.marxists.org/admin/books/manifesto/Manifesto.pdf.

[10] Valdman, "A Theory of Wrongful Exploitation."

[11] S. White, *The Civic Minimum* (New York, 2003), 44. Cited by Valdman, "A Theory of Wrongful Exploitation," 9.

increases in virtue of some kind of offer to transact, work, or co-
operate. For instance, in a coercion case where the coercer points
a gun at his victim and shouts, "Your money or your life!" the
coercer's action functions to add a new constraint to the coercee's
original state of affairs, thereby decreasing the coercee's overall set
of rational options.[12]

Conversely, if a drowning man can be easily saved by his friend
and his friend offers to toss him a life preserver but only on the
condition that he promises to give him $100,000, then the friend's
actions function to increase the drowning victim's overall set of
options. Thus, exploitation cases are often, all things considered
though counterintuitively, mutually beneficial to both parties and
often occur with the informed consent of the exploitee. What's
more, relative to the cost of not transacting at all, the exploitee often
benefits considerably more so than the supposed exploiter from the
interaction. Hence, pinning down just what exactly is intuitively
morally problematic about the phenomenon of exploitation turns
out, perhaps surprisingly, to be quite difficult theoretically.

Vulnerability

One common feature among many contemporary theories of exploitation is the notion of exploitee *vulnerability*. Indeed, along with
the concept of exploiter benefit, this concept of exploitee vulnerability seems indispensable to any working theory of exploitation.
What's more, according to many popular exploitation accounts,
the degree to which an agent is vulnerable will often play a decisive role in determining whether something should count as a case
of harmful exploitation versus mutually beneficial exploitation.

---

[12] While exploitation is distinct from closely related concepts such as coercion and
oppression, exploitation can also be comorbid with and constitutive of coercion and oppression. For instance, slavery is an instance of oppression and coercion, but it is also
often or usually exploitative as well.

Hence, a particular case might still count as exploitation, but without sufficient vulnerability on the part of the exploitee, the relative difference in emergent benefits distributed between exploiter and exploitee might fail to be severe enough to make the exploitee sufficiently "worse off" relative to some baseline of fairness or objective well-being.

Conceptions of vulnerability have varied among theorists, ranging from formulations like those proposed by Alan Wertheimer to more stringent formulations like those offered by Mikhail Valdman. For Wertheimer, an agent is vulnerable to exploitation if she is under pressure because of the urgency and severity of a decision-making situation and/or if she is lacking adequate information.[13] For Valdman, an agent is vulnerable if she lacks adequate information to make an informed decision or is completely out of reasonable options.[14]

On Wertheimer's view, a worker could freely and knowingly *choose* to allow himself to be exploited if doing so would improve his financial situation on balance despite his full knowledge of the excessive or unfair distribution of the cooperative surplus generated by the transaction with the exploiter. Accordingly, on Wertheimer's view, the worker could be morally blameworthy for choosing to allow himself to be exploited in such a way, especially if his actions were deleterious to the bargaining efforts of his fellow disenfranchised workers. On Valdman's view, however, the exploitee *cannot* choose, of his own volition, to allow himself to be exploited. Indeed, Valdman concedes that perhaps he can choose to "let himself be used," but in such cases, according to Valdman, the agent will not technically be exploited since *not* opting into the unfair transaction will still be among the set of "reasonable" alternatives available to him.[15]

---

[13] Wertheimer, *Exploitation*.
[14] Valdman, "A Theory of Wrongful Exploitation."
[15] Valdman, "A Theory of Wrongful Exploitation," 9.

However, if the worker has a starving family and he has no other reasonable option but to acquiesce to the demands of the employer or risk being fired, then, according to Valdman, the worker would not be freely choosing to allow himself to be used.[16] Rather, the worker would be in a situation of being exploited in virtue of his total absence of reasonable options. Importantly, in such a case then, unlike on Wertheimer's view, it would be conceptually impossible for the exploited party to be morally blameworthy for his decision to participate in the exploitative transaction. As Valdman puts it for an agent to genuinely and legitimately be vulnerable, she must "have her back to the wall," so to speak. In consideration of this claim, we may ask, how should we understand the scope and ways in which an agent can be said to truly be "out of reasonable options"?

To help us answer this question, take Valdman's "Antidote" case, for example, one which is regularly offered as a paradigmatic example of exploitation. This is an important case both in the broader exploitation literature and for our main argument on moral exploitation later in the book. The case runs as follows:

> Two hikers, Hiker A and Hiker B are walking in the woods when Hiker A is bitten by a poisonous snake. Hiker A needs immediate aid or else he will die. Fortunately for Hiker A, Hiker B has the $10 antidote. However, rather than just giving it to him, Hiker B demands $10,000 from Hiker A in exchange for the antidote. Left with very few options, Hiker A agrees to Hiker B's demands. The transaction occurs and both hikers exit the woods having

---

[16] There is a further important question here: Can an exploitee unknowingly be exploited? We believe that one can, and it is perhaps more common than often thought. Amartya Sen's discussion about the diminished agency and adaptive preference of abused women could be a potential example or starting point for thinking through this form of unknown (to the exploitee) exploitation. See Sen, *Poverty and Famines* (Oxford, 1981). We will return to this question later in the book. A further question is whether an exploiter can unknowingly exploit others. Again, we believe this can and does occur, and it helps explain some of the large, societal exploitative features we explore in this book.

mutually benefited, Hiker A having benefited considerably more so than Hiker B relative to the cost of not transacting at all.[17]

Here we clearly see Hiker B exploiting Hiker A by leveraging a pronounced physical constraint that is serving to close off Hiker A's set of reasonable options. Valdman argues that the Antidote case exemplifies a paradigmatic instance of (wrongful) exploitation since it possesses the dual characteristics of (1) excessive gain on the part of the exploiter, and (2) a total lack of reasonable options on the part of the exploitee. For Valdman this is critical, since nothing short of one having her back to the wall and being completely out of reasonable options would count as being vulnerable in the needed sense. Accordingly, on Valdman's view, people cannot reasonably *choose* to be exploited, because that entails that they still had reasonable options available to them.

Contrary to Valdman, Alan Wertheimer offers a less stringent notion of exploitee vulnerability. According to Wertheimer, an agent is vulnerable, not only in extreme cases when she "has her back to the wall" but also when she is under pressure and not well informed.[18] Hence, on Wertheimer's view, an agent can be legitimately vulnerable while still having reasonable options available to her and can sometimes choose to be exploited of her own volition. In his influential work, *Exploitation*, Wertheimer's set of specific exploitation cases includes the exploitation of female commercial surrogates for their surrogacy services, the exploitation of student-athletes by universities for their athletic performance, and the exploitation of patients by psychotherapists for sex.[19]

In the case of student-athletes exploited by universities for their athletic performance, some combination of economic and emotional vulnerability, according to Wertheimer, is often present.

---

[17] Mikhail Valdman, 'Exploitation and Injustice,' *Social Theory and Practice*, 34, no. 4 (2008), 551–572.
[18] Wertheimer, *Exploitation*.
[19] Wertheimer, *Exploitation*.

Indeed, in many US colleges and universities across the country, student-athletes are often recruited from economically disadvantaged backgrounds and also have strong hopes of either "making it" as professional athletes or, at the very least, acquiring a university degree with the corresponding educational skill set commensurate with such a degree. According to Wertheimer, the large social surplus generated from the transaction, in the form of monetary revenue and social capital, often gets unfairly or excessively distributed to the university while only a fraction of it is seen by the student-athlete. The student-athletes on the other hand, many of who will not have their hopes and dreams of becoming professional athletes come true, will often come away from the exchange with a college education that is severely lacking, either because of the disproportionate amount of time spent on the playing field or because, from the very beginning, they were knowingly recruited from a place where actual uptake of such university-level knowledge was never really likely.[20] This last point is pertinent as it will be directly relevant to our analysis of military recruitment in Chapter 2. In that chapter, we examine how military recruitment incentives in the form of promised job skills contrast with the actual data on pervasive veteran unemployment and job retention.

With respect to the exploitation of patients by psychotherapists for sex, Wertheimer notes the pronounced emotional vulnerability that is often present in such cases. Given the psychologist's expert knowledge, the patient often lets her emotional guard down and shares deeply personal features about herself, things she would not otherwise share with any other person were it not for the psychologist's unique medical role. Oftentimes, it is not uncommon in such circumstances for patients to mistake this emotional sharing (and the psychologist's listening and comforting) with romantic attachment. The patient is, in effect, putting herself in a place of extreme emotional vulnerability as well as in a

---

[20] Wertheimer, *Exploitation*.

place where there is a pronounced asymmetric power differential between the two. Sometimes therapists take unfair advantage of this emotional vulnerability and leverage it for unfair romantic or sexual gain. While none of Wertheimer's cases meet Valdman's more stringent criteria for an agent being out of reasonable options in a "back to the wall" sense, they nonetheless admit of a general pattern whereby the agent's reasonable options are restricted by some economic, emotional, or trust-based constraint.

In addition to Wertheimer, other philosophers have offered more expansive accounts of vulnerability and have noted how trust-based relationships can also be a legitimate source of exploitation. Hallie Liberto, for instances, gives a case involving a minister taking advantage of the special trust relationship between himself and one of the members of his congregation in order to sell him a piece of bad real-estate property for an exceptionally high price.[21] In this particular case, the minister unfairly leverages the special trust his congregation member places in him as minister to gain personal advantage in another domain which he knows little or nothing about. Elsewhere, in "Noxious Markets versus Noxious Gift-Relationships," Liberto argues that within the special context of friendship, both parties knowingly take the other person's interests into account when making decisions.[22] Accordingly, there is a tacit understanding between both parties to refrain from "playing hardball" and attempting to maximize one's own interests. Liberto thereby acknowledges the action-constraining features generated by one's moral and trust-based commitments with regard to friends, friendship, and special relations.

Similarly, in *Exploiting a Situation and Exploiting a Person,* Robert Goodin presents several cases where an agent's set of trust-based commitments function as an additional constraint closing

---

[21] Hallie Liberto, "Noxious Markets versus Noxious Gift Relationships," *Social Theory and Practice*, 39, no. 2 (2013), 265–287.
[22] Liberto, "Noxious Markets versus Noxious Gift Relationships."

off her set of reasonable options, therefore making her legitimately vulnerable.[23] In one example, Goodin offers a case where a group of co-workers exploit their hard-working peer who is considerably more invested in a collaborative group project. Knowing full well their peer's deep sense of obligation and investment in the success of the project, the other workers choose to neglect their duties during the project, confident their hard-working peer will pick up the slack. One entailment of Goodin's case is an acknowledgment that *moral convictions*, just like physical, economic, or epistemic constraints, can serve as a source of legitimate vulnerability and can sometimes dramatically constrain an agent's reasonable options. Considerations of moral convictions, as well as moral interactions more broadly, will play heavily into our account in this chapter. We might wonder, for example, if a citizen's sense of duty to nation might function similarly.

Mutually Beneficial Exploitation, Harmful Exploitation, and Baselines

Benefit

Aside from the various notions of vulnerability just canvassed, another key thought as to a necessary feature of exploitation—and on some accounts like Valdman's it is indeed *the* unique wrong-making feature of exploitation—is the idea of excessive or unfair exploiter benefit.[24] During an interaction or transaction between two persons (or groups), so the thought goes, some kind of cooperative or social surplus is generated on account of the transaction that did not exist beforehand. The degree to which that cooperative surplus is then fairly apportioned or distributed between parties,

---

[23] Goodin, 1985.
[24] Valdman, "A Theory of Wrongful Exploitation," 3.

on some accounts, will then determine, at least in part, whether a transaction should count as exploitative and, furthermore, whether that transaction should count as an instance of *mutually* beneficial versus *harmful* exploitation.[25] Hence, a transaction may be exploitative when indexed to the fair market price yet on balance mutually beneficial and non-harmful to the exploitee when indexed to the baseline of objective well-being, such as in Valdman's Antidote case. Alternatively, if Hiker B demanded a sex act, say, from Hiker A in exchange for the antidote, then the transaction would be both exploitative and harmful in objective well-being sense.

Transactional versus Relational Exploitation

Another important feature of exploitation is the form it takes. Broadly speaking, cases of exploitation tend to take the form of either a discrete transaction or of an ongoing relation. This transactional/relational distinction, as we will soon see, proves vital in our understanding of the moral exploitation of soldiers that we will explore at length in Chapter 2. With respect to transactional exploitation, a common example would be something like the one-time exchange of a commodity on the free market where the seller of that commodity garnered excessive value from the buyer relative to the baseline of the "fair market price."

With respect to ongoing relational exploitation, three major kinds arguably obtain depending on size and scale. For example, a small-scale instance of relational exploitation would be something

---

[25] It is not obvious though that the emergent cooperative surplus needs to always be homogeneous and/or cleanly divisible in such an easily described manner. Indeed, the emergent surplus could be heterogenous and/or multifaceted as well as indivisible. For instance, consider a business relationship where one partner naturally tends to take the lead while the other might have a natural inclination to assisting. This could arguably be done in a complementary way that is mutually respectful, non-exploitative, and equitable. What's more the aggregate emergent good that came out of such a division of labor (i.e., a business) might be equally worth the interaction for both sides.

like an exploitative romantic relationship. Indeed, within movies as well as real life, we have likely seen instances where an ongoing power dynamic existed between romantic partners whereby one partner clearly gained excessively at the other's expense. Ongoing instances of relational exploitation, however, can arguably obtain at a scale beyond just interpersonal dynamics. For instance, mid-tier forms of relational exploitation can also exist between groups and/ or within small and mid-scale institutions. Wertheimer's cases of the ongoing exploitative relationship between colleges and student-athletes, for instance, or between commercial surrogacy companies and commercial surrogates seem to exemplify this mid-tier form. Lastly, ongoing relational exploitation seems to obtain at large-scale institutional or societal/structural levels as well. The claim of capitalism's exploitation of the working class, for instance, would be an example of just such a large-scale structural form of relational exploitation.[26]

An important point to note regarding this transactional/relational distinction is that transactional exploitation can sometimes lead into relational forms of exploitation but not always. For instance, an initially exploitative offer/transaction can lead into an ongoing exploitative relationship between the commercial surrogate and the surrogacy company/family. Conversely, an initially non-exploitative interaction can be the founding moment that forms a romantic relationship that becomes exploitative at a later point in time. As we will see in Chapter 2, the initial recruitment offer between recruits and the military body and the ongoing structural relationship between soldiers and society at large will admit both of these overlapping transactional and relational elements.

---

[26] Note that we are not saying here that Marx's theory is correct, only that his claims about capital and labor exemplify an instance of exploitation taken to the large-scale level of institutions and structures.

Contexts and Background Conditions

Closely related to this latter point about relational exploitation taking the form of large-scale institutions and/or structures is the much broader question of contexts and background conditions. Indeed, arguably all the conceptual machinery we have referenced so far in our analysis of exploitation, concepts like vulnerability, reasonable options, sufficient information, fairness, baselines, benefit, harm, negligence, personal responsibility, respect, and more, will have to be indexed to some assumed set of background conditions if it is to be fully coherent. To see this, return to Valdman's Antidote case. There Valdman claims that such a case is an exemplar of wrongful exploitation since it involves both the canonical elements of excessive exploiter benefit and an exploitee being completely out of reasonable options. This is not intuitively obvious, however, without us projecting or filling in, to some extent, a certain set of assumed background conditions pertaining to the "commonsense world" that the two hikers are operating in.

Are the two hikers hiking in an otherwise "normal" state park or are they knowingly hiking in the notoriously dangerous Snake Canyon? Is this a one-off case or an iterative case where Hiker A has forgotten his antidote for the twelfth consecutive time? Is Hiker A Bill Gates or Jeff Bezos? Did this same scenario happen a year prior only in reverse and this is now a case of reciprocal pay back? Is Hiker A a member of a group traditionally exploited by the members of a group which Hiker B belongs to?[27]

While a full treatment of these questions goes well beyond the scope of this chapter, and indeed, beyond the scope of this book, it

---

[27] Indeed, stipulations of ceteris paribus, or "all things being equal," does little here to bracket these concerns since the case itself still leaves much of the background context underdetermined. Such underdetermination then allows for readers to project their own subjective assumptions about risk, personal responsibility, negligence, etc. to fill in the gaps. Given such a state of affairs, it is not obvious then, in such cases, what exactly is pumping our intuitions; reasons related to exploitation in particular or projected background assumptions.

is worth highlighting here that the question of what significance (if any) the elements of context and historical backstory in particular ought to play in our overall moral assessment of distinct exploitation cases. Just how contextually or historically sensitive our treatment of independent exploitation cases can or ought to ultimately be, we leave open, since a full theory would require significant fleshing out of, among other things, deep metaphysical and moral commitments pertaining to all of the following: justice and reparative justice; liability and desert; morally relevant counterfactuals and comparison classes; theories about how groups persist and perdure over time; and the transitivity of properties of groups to individual persons.[28] We nonetheless explicitly acknowledge that such writ large considerations will be humming in the background of the theories of exploitation we have here discussed as well as our own.

Objections

Thus far we have noted how notions of exploitation differ from notions of coercion, how different philosophers have cashed out the concepts of agent vulnerability and agent benefit, what distinguishes mutually beneficial from harmful exploitation, the difference between transactional and relational exploitation, and how we should regard various structural and historical background conditions. We have yet, however, to explore the moral significance of cases of exploitation relative to cases of neglect. Indeed, a strong argument advanced by libertarian philosopher, Matt Zwolinski, argues that presumptively bad exploitation cases aren't as morally bad as we might initially think when we consider how exploitation trades off against the comparison class of mere neglect. We can summarize his argument roughly as follows.

---

[28] Such background considerations similarly effect any working theory of oppression.

Mere neglect is, all things considered, morally worse than exploitation, since any exploitative exchange necessarily increases the set of overall options a vulnerable party possesses prior to the exploitative offer. Hence, on this view, sweatshops that exploitatively recruit and employ vulnerable persons actually do something morally *less* wrong than institutional arrangements, persons, and groups that neglect vulnerable persons entirely and offer them no options of employment at all. To spell this out, imagine that A is in a vulnerable position and B offers A an exploitative offer that will improve A's predicament, but only suboptimally relative to the full set of ways B could potentially help A. Meanwhile, C does nothing at all to affect A's predicament. Comparatively, then, it seems that B is actually doing something more morally praiseworthy or, at least, less morally blameworthy than C's complete neglect of A's vulnerable predicament. Accordingly, it seems that the charge that B is doing something wrong because "he isn't doing enough" to help A ends up more severely condemning C who does absolutely nothing to interact with A. Or so argues Zwolinksi.

As Zwolinski points out, consideration of such a case then generates the counterintuitive conclusion that the majority of people in the world are doing something morally worse than sweatshop owners by refraining from owning and operating sweatshops and opting instead to offer nothing to impoverished people at all.[29] The claim is that our initial intuitions about the wrongness of sweatshops are simply erroneous because we often conflate too quickly our visceral gut instincts having to do with the impoverished background conditions of the sweatshop workers relative to our first-world living conditions. What is less considered or popularized within the social imagination, Zwolinski points out, are the even worse and more impoverished conditions that

---

[29] For Zwolinski's treatment of exploitation see, Matt Zwolinski, "Sweatshops, Choice, and Exploitation," *Philosophy: Faculty Scholarship*, 17 (2007), 690; and idem, "Structural Exploitation," *Social Philosophy and Policy*, 29, no. 1 (2012), 154–179.

sweatshop workers came from prior to the sweatshop's creation. We admit that this is a fair point and worth remembering: As heinous and awful as sweatshop labor is, for many of those who are exploited by them, working in a sweatshop might actually be a better life than other alternatives or their life before the sweatshop.

Zwolinski's challenge can therefore be summarized as follows: Either exploitation is seriously wrong and neglect is even more seriously wrong (on account that the exploiter actually offers something to improve the vulnerable person's predicament while the neglector offers nothing) or, alternatively, neglect isn't that morally wrong but then neither really is exploitation. Independent of the overall appraisal of the moral severity of either neglect or exploitation, Zwolinksi's key point is that the positional relationship between neglect and exploitation remains constant, with neglect always being morally worse than exploitation, all things considered.[30]

For many, the force of Zwolinski's argument will largely come down to one's prior philosophical commitments concerning two important moral concepts: autonomy and well-being. How these two moral features are weighted, as well as how they trade off against one another, do most of the work here for most people's intuitions on this view. For someone who has an exceptionally libertarian commitment to the maximization of autonomy, Zwolinski's neglect challenge will quite likely succeed and make it the case that offering an exploitative deal to a rational agent will be morally less bad than not offering any deal at all. If, however, one has more substantive commitments to notions of objective well-being, then offering an exploitative set of options that will foreseeably make an autonomous agent's life objectively worse could then count as morally worse than mere neglect. Selling high-interest payday loans or lottery tickets to homeless people, for instance, might be a good

---

[30] For a lengthy debate about exploitation, neglect, and the limits of markets, see Matt Zwolinski and Debra Satz, "Where Are the Moral Lines of Markets?," YouTube, April 6, 2016, https://www.youtube.com/watch?v=WBd2s0D8akI.

example of such a case. Even though one is technically giving more options to such vulnerable persons and ostensibly "honoring their autonomy" as rational adults to make their own decisions, it still seems it is morally worse in these cases to offer such options to vulnerable persons since to provide such options will predictably (and quite reliably predictably) make their lives objectively worse in the long run. Accordingly, on a stronger view of objective well-being, the morally less wrong action would be to neglect the homeless person rather than offer an exploitative option that would predictably make worse their already precarious situation. Note that one can give significant weight to objective well-being and embrace the significant moral importance of autonomy as well—the two need not be mutually exclusive or necessarily in conflict.[31]

Lastly, one might think, as does Debra Satz, that there is something about the particular market itself and the type of commodity being exchanged that should affect our overall moral appraisal of different exploitation versus neglect cases. If our theory of neglect and exploitation is indeed sensitive to such considerations, then Zwolinski's claim about the static positional relationship between neglect and exploitation might no longer hold. In other words, the moral severity of exploitation versus neglect might yield different results for markets involving bags of ice versus markets involving vital organs or child labor. That being said, we might then wonder how we should morally appraise exploitation versus neglect cases involving transfer of the "good" of moral responsibility. We will tackle that key question shortly.

---

[31] Exploring such discussions of the weight and value of autonomy, however, is well beyond our scope here. This is a huge topic in normative ethics expansively covered by many theorists. We have written about the importance of autonomy and how that value can be respected alongside other values. See, Strawser, *Bounds of Defense* (forthcoming from OUP). For other sources on autonomy, see X, Y, and Z. Additionally, it is worth mentioning that some may here have worries of paternalism when we weight others' objective well-being alongside their autonomy as guiding or moral deliberation on how it is best to treat them. The paternalism worry is not unimportant, but, again, we believe one can weight others' objective well-being while simultaneously respecting their autonomy.

Unique Wrongness

Given what we have said about exploitation, we might now ask: *What exactly is the unique wrongness of exploitation?* Let us turn now to examine several plausible candidates.

Instrumental Use

Some philosophers might conclude that the unique wrongness of exploitation comes down to an exploiter's instrumental use of an exploitee. Indeed, anyone with Kantian or deontological leanings might find such an analysis persuasive. On Kant's view, to use someone as a *mere means* constitutes a wronging of that person. Using someone's vulnerability for excessive gain arguably constitutes an instance of using someone as a mere means and thereby could constitute wronging someone in this way. Allen Wood goes further with this notion, contending that the special wrong-making feature of exploitation is not merely the instrumental use of a person, but, more specifically, the instrumental use of a person's vulnerability. To further our own ends by intentionally targeting another's specific vulnerability, Wood argues, is degrading to that individual and hence is the hallmark of exploitation's unique wrongness. Going further still is Robert Goodin who argues that the special wrongness of exploitation comes as a result of not only failing to uphold a fundamental positive duty to assist those who are vulnerable but also then turning that vulnerability to our own advantage. All of these accounts might therefore capture what it is we find intuitively problematic about exploitation cases.

Fairness

Another explanation addressing exploitation's unique wrongness might have something to do with fairness. In all cases of exploitation, the exploitee is in some sense made better off relative to the baseline of not transacting at all. However, many philosophers working on exploitation challenge the notion that the counterfactual case of "not transacting at all" should be the proper moral baseline that we should focus on. Indeed, rather than focusing on the baseline of non-transaction, some philosophers argue that we should instead index our thinking to a "fair market price" baseline for cases of economic transactions or to some other baseline of fairness (perhaps having to do with objective well-being) for non-economic transactions. The comparative gulf between an exploitee's vulnerability (as indexed to this baseline) and an exploiter's excessive benefit (as indexed to this baseline) might then tell us the overall severity of how exploitative a given transaction or relationship is.

Respect

In addition to explanations having to do with instrumental use or fairness, we alternatively think that the unique wrongness of exploitation instead comes down to something having to do with respect. Both Goodin's and Wood's accounts of exploitation's unique wrongness mentioned briefly earlier seem to gesture at this notion. Hence, rather than explaining the wrongness of exploitation in terms of using someone as a mere means or in terms of the creation of a type of unfairness (market based or otherwise), we might instead conclude that exploitation is uniquely wrong insofar as it fails to satisfy a basic duty of treating persons with a certain degree of proper human respect. Indeed, there arguably seems to be a certain indignity to things like sweatshop labor and sex work even when persons are compensated generously. This felt sense of a lack of respect for exploitees might also closely track with special duties of respect for person's bodily autonomy. In any event, such moral considerations seem to function independently from just instrumental use or fairness considerations.

Second-Order Effects

Aside from these primary explanations, other scholars might suspect what is uniquely wrong with exploitation is that it generates deleterious second-order effects to the objective well-being of individuals and greater society. Debra Satz, for instance, argues that markets can become "noxious" when they consist of four elements: vulnerability, weak agency, deleterious consequences to individuals, and deleterious consequences to society at large.[32] Hence, on Satz's view, this gives us good reason for the state to limit such noxious markets from existing and propagating. While such a view arguably might not deal with wrongness of exploitation as such, these downstream consequences of exploitation might still be closely enough associated with cases of exploitation to warrant ethical concern and certain positive duties.

Incommensurability

A final explanation addressing the unique wrongness of exploitation comes from Michael Walzer. Walzer suggests that cases we would intuitively want to deem as "exploitative" have something to with the (attempted) exchange of fundamentally incommensurable kinds of goods; what he refers to as "blocked exchanges."[33] Hence, in Walzer's view, if there is no point of commensurability or parity whereby different kinds of goods can be metaphysically exchanged, then this gives us reason to think that there's something wrong going on. This point about the incommensurability of different goods will have significant relevance for our consideration of

---

[32] Debra Satz, *Why Some Things Should Not Be for Sale: The Moral Limits of Markets* (New York, 2010).
[33] See Michael Walzer, *Spheres of Justice: A Defense of Pluralism and Equality* (New York, 1983).

the exchange or transfer of moral duties and moral responsibilities later in this chapter.

While this capturing of accounts isn't meant to be exhaustive, it at least captures some of the major explanations as to exploitation's unique wrongness. As a note to the reader, we do not commit ourselves to any one account here nor do we rule out the possibility that exploitation's wrongness might indeed be overdetermined by a variety of these factors.

Moral Implications

As a final point, we will now consider just what is the moral significance and moral implications of exploitation. More specifically, we might ask: *Where on the moral ledger ought we situate exploitation relative to other moral considerations? And, What normative pushes and pulls does the existence of exploitation generate?*

In terms of moral significance, prima facie we might think that exploitation does not rank as high in severity as other close normative cousins such as coercion, abuse, and oppression since there seems to be a volitional component to exploitation that is not present in these other cases. Hence, relative to these comparison classes, it seems all things considered morally preferable to offer someone an exploitative offer versus letting them be coerced, abused, or oppressed, but still suboptimal to offering them a non-exploitative offer. Along these same lines, we might also think that, ceteris paribus, it might be morally better to offer someone a somewhat exploitative offer when they are faced with the choice of having to accept a more exploitative offer from someone else, yet still morally worse that offering them a non-exploitative offer.

With respect to normative implications, the existence of exploitation intuitively seems to generate duties that parse into ex ante and ex post considerations respectively. In terms of ex ante duties, the likelihood of exploitation might engender personal duties to not "play for advantage" against persons who are noticeably vulnerable as well as epistemic duties to suss out whether a person is potentially vulnerable before transacting. Similarly, in terms of collective duties, the likelihood of exploitation might engender duties to a society to constrain certain markets and market transactions to prevent instances of exploitation as well as to prevent downstream negative second-order effects and "noxious" markets from occurring. In terms of ex post considerations, the presence of exploitation could generate corresponding duties of compensation, depending on the specifics of the situation and what other comparative options were available at the time, and depending on whether it was a case of mutually beneficial versus harmful exploitation.

Synopsis

To be clear, the synopsis of standard instances and definitions of exploitation we have given here is not intended to be exhaustive or complete. Rather, our main goal is to show the reader the major working conceptual parts of various contemporary exploitation accounts and to use these accounts to better explain, in this chapter and in later chapters, what we take to be one of the morally troubling elements of the present-day soldier's relationship to the state and to civilian society at large. Importantly, unlike these standard accounts that all exclusively cash out exploitation in terms of an unfair exchange of a physical good, service, or commodity between exploiter and exploitee, we make the further claim that duty and moral responsibility can serve among the set of things unfairly exchanged or distributed during an exploitative transaction or relationship. Let us now explore what exactly we mean by this.

Moral Exploitation

Consider the following scenario.[34] Anna is Beth's boss. One day, because of budgetary cuts within the company, Anna is faced with the difficult decision of having to suddenly fire one of two employees to save the future of the entire company. In other words, she must break a pro tanto contractual obligation for the sake of the all-things-considered good of the company's survival. Both of these employees are excellent workers who have spent equal time with the company and both of them have an important reason for not wanting to be fired. One worker is a single mother of three. The other is trying to raise money for his wife's chemotherapy. Not wanting to have to deal with the psychological duress of moral deliberation that would go into making such a difficult decision and not wanting to be potentially blameworthy for making the wrong decision, Anna decides to delegate the responsibility of firing one of these two employees to Beth in exchange for a promotion that will lift Beth out of the ranks of people who are being considered for upcoming layoffs. Anna knows that Beth will accept since Beth is in dire need of job security. For the sake of argument, let us also assume that this new responsibility falls well outside of Beth's normal and originally agreed upon job description. Anna proceeds to task Beth with this new responsibility, and Beth accepts without resistance.

In examining this case, we may note, that by transacting with Anna, Beth takes on three new and distinct "moral burdens," or at least three potential burdens, that she did not have prior to the transaction. First, by agreeing to Anna's proposal, Beth takes on a new and distinct moral deliberative role, one outside the purview of her expected job requirements, and one which entails new psychological stresses she did not have before. Second, Beth takes on

---

[34] Much of this section can be understood as a further fleshing out and advancement of our earlier writings surrounding the phenomenon of moral exploitation.

new moral risks associated with this deliberative role, along with potential blameworthiness. Third, by being placed in this situation, Beth risks making the wrong moral decision and thereby incurring some degree of moral residue, or "dirty hands."

Borrowing from Judith Jarvis Thomson, moral residue occurs in instances where one is obligated to infringe a pro tanto right in order to promote the all-things-considered good. To understand this notion of moral residue, consider Fienberg's classic Cabin Case. Suppose A and B are hiking in the secluded woods when they are both caught in a freak blizzard. B begins to demonstrate signs of hypothermia and will die soon unless he is immediately brought to warmth and shelter. Fortunately for B, there is an unused locked cabin nearby. With no time to get B to a hospital, A kicks in the door of the cabin and uses the cabin's furniture for firewood to bring B's core temperature back to normal and thus saving him.[35]

Under otherwise normal circumstances, most people would think that A has a pro tanto duty to observe the property rights of the cabin owner. Were it not an emergency rescue scenario, and A just wanted to break into the cabin for fun, then such an act, on Thomson's view, would constitute a rights violation of the cabin owner. However, given the dire circumstances of the case described, most people would think that A has an all-things-considered duty to save B's life that trumps his pro tanto duty to respect the cabin owner's right to personal property. Such a scenario would therefore constitute a case of rights infringement as opposed to a rights violation. Despite A having an all-things-considered moral obligation to save B's life (and to therefore infringe the pro tanto property rights of the cabin owner as an unintended but necessary and foreseeable side effect), Thomson argues that A's morally obligatory actions generate moral residue, or dirty hands.[36] This moral residue

---

[35] Joel Feinberg, *Rights, Justice, and the Bounds of Liberty* (New Jersey, 1980), 221–225.
[36] See Judith Jarvis Thomson, "Self-Defense and Rights," in *Rights, Restitution and Risk*, ed. W. A. Parent (1986), 37.

uniquely attaches to A whereby A incurs an ex post duty to the cabin owner in the form of compensation for infringing the cabin owner's pro tanto property rights. In the case of Anna and Beth, an argument can be made that Anna leverage's Beth's vulnerability not only to distance and insulate herself from the moral deliberation and moral risks associated with the high-stakes decision-making context but also to ensure that any foreseeable moral residue attaches to Beth and not to herself with respect to breaking the pro tanto contract with the fired worker.

Exploitation's "Currency"

As previously noted, on standard exploitation accounts, one person, A, extracts an excessive or unfair benefit from another person, B. Importantly, in such exploitation cases, the unfair extraction is made possible by B's pronounced vulnerability. What's more, in many standard cases within the exploitation literature, the thing being unfairly moved or transferred between exploiter and exploitee—the *currency* of exploitation, as we will call it here—is often tacitly presumed to take the form of some kind of tangible good or service (e.g., money, sexual services, physical labor) that is moved from exploitee to exploiter. This account of exploitation's currency is too narrow however. Acquisition of a physical good or service does not exhaust the ways a person can be said to unfairly benefit or have his or her state of affairs be comparatively improved. Indeed, exploiter benefit, in the case described in the previous section, does not take the form of the acquisition of a particular physical good or physical service but rather takes the form of a kind of distancing from or insulation from having to make hard moral decisions or having to take on additional moral responsibility, moral risk, or the increased likelihood of dirty hands.

In the case of Anna, she benefits from the exploitative transaction by no longer having to concern herself with the specific deliberative moral decision of which employee to keep and which one to let go. Nor does she have to deal with the moral risk of getting it wrong. Nor does she have to deal with the potential of incurring any moral residue.

Spelled out explicitly then:

> Moral exploitation involves cases where an exploiter takes unfair advantage of an exploitee's vulnerability, not to gain any sort of physical good or service but rather to leverage the exploitee's vulnerability such that the agent agrees to accept additional or excessive moral burdens (i.e., moral deliberative roles, moral risk, and/ or moral residue) that she would not otherwise accept were she not vulnerable.

In effect, the exploiter benefits from this transaction by outsourcing responsibility and duties onto the exploitee and thereby distancing herself from the proximity of a given decision-making context and its concomitant moral burdens.

Understanding that the currency of exploitation can take the form of not only an unfair or disproportionate distribution of a physical good or service but also an unfair or disproportionate distribution of moral burdens is no small matter. If our conception of exploitation's currency remains restricted to just physical goods and services then, in terms of our moral prescriptions ex ante, our focus will likely be restricted to preventing and being on the lookout for only those scenarios where a physical good or service might be unfairly exchanged. Likewise, in terms of our moral prescriptions ex post, our ideas of proper corrective or compensatory measures will likely be confined to only notions involving a redistribution of exclusively physical commodities between exploiter and exploitee. If, however, a case does *not* display this feature of a recognizable physical transfer of a good or service, then the unsaid conclusion, it would then seem, is that what we are looking at is not exploitation and therefore not warranting of similar preventative and corrective measures. The tacit implication is that if there is no unfair distribution of goods and services that might foreseeably occur, then there's nothing to prevent in terms of exploitation. Likewise, if physical goods and services are appropriately redistributed after an exploitative act, then the exploitation is presumed to have stopped. Both conclusions, we contend, are false.

It is important to note here that we are not committing ourselves to any one specific theory of exploitation. Indeed, our notion of moral burdens as a legitimate currency of exploitation can be paired with exploitation accounts like Valdman's, which require that an agent must be out of all reasonable options to be considered vulnerable, or with less stringent accounts, like Wertheimer's, which simply require that a vulnerable agent be under pressure or lacking relevant information. What's more, we believe that this idea of moral exploitation is compatible with accounts that formulate exploitation as sometimes mutually beneficial, consensual or non-consensual, or necessarily or contingently involving the unfair distribution of a generated social surplus.

Like standard cases of exploitation, in cases of moral exploitation, the exploitee is usually, all things considered, made better off relative to not transacting at all. However, just like in cases of standard exploitation, in cases of moral exploitation, what the exploitee ultimately gains is unfairly disproportionate to what the exploiter gains (or tries to gain) from the transaction. And while the exploiter does not technically gain any sort of physical good or service during a morally exploitative act, what the exploiter does gain is a sort of escape or distancing from the set of moral burdens that he effectively passes on to the exploitee to bear. In this way, the feature of an unfair or excessive gain/benefit on the part of the exploiter is still very much present in cases of moral exploitation but manifested somewhat differently when compared to standard exploitation examples.

In cases of moral exploitation, in many respects, the exploitee's agency often becomes more constrained in virtue of her taking on these new moral burdens. However, it is worth noting that in other respects, the exploitee's agency may be technically enhanced. In this way it is possible that persons in institutional leadership roles can also be morally exploited. Given the exploitative exchange and lopsided distribution of moral burdens, Beth is also endowed with a new power and capacity to make a decision she was not previously able to make. What's more, we can also imagine a case where Beth would gain certain incentives within the company (i.e., higher pay, faster career progression, etc.) were she to take on the responsibility of firing one of her fellow employees. But these gains are still in keeping with the proposal that Beth is wrongly exploited. After all, standard exploitation cases usually involve gains to an exploitee. Indeed, that is why most exploited persons knowingly consent to their own exploitation. The issue then is not that Beth doesn't gain at all from the transaction. Rather, it is that Anna gains disproportionately at Beth's expense.

Accordingly, Anna still morally exploits Beth. This is so precisely because there has been an unfair imposition of a set of moral burdens upon a vulnerable agent, who, because of her vulnerability, likely could not have refused to accept such burdens regardless of the accompanying benefits. Hence, even though Beth's agency is all things considered enhanced by the exploitative exchange, she is nonetheless wronged, if only in a pro tanto sense, given that the deliberative role was ultimately placed upon her unfairly and excessively. The degree of unfairness here seems to be at least partially tracked by the degree to which the new responsibility unfairly thrust upon her diverges from the role (and concomitant responsibilities) she originally consented to shoulder. The wrongness of moral exploitation then has something to do perhaps with the divergence between the understood responsibilities associated with one's initially agreed upon role and the hidden, latent, or manifest responsibilities that develop with that role over time.

Bearing this point in mind, moral exploitation we can therefore see as further dividing into two major types. The first, more common type involves an unfair offloading of some kind of deliberative role from exploiter to exploitee, but not, as it were, an actual *transferring* of concomitant moral responsibility. To see this, consider the borderline case of the baby at the doorstep. Imagine that in the middle of the night someone leaves a newborn baby on your doorstep, rings your doorbell, and runs away. In doing so, we do not think the person's physical offloading of the newborn child has resulted in an actual offloading of the accompanying moral responsibility for caring for the child.

Experientially, it might very well seem to the person, from his extremely selfish perspective, that he is fully off the hook in terms of responsibility to the child. He might even be able to sleep more soundly at night because of this, but he would simply be mistaken as to what his responsibilities actually were. Indeed, his duties to the child would still very much obtain. He would just be failing miserably in upholding them. Nonetheless, when you open your door to discover the newborn baby, regardless of the fact that the responsibility for that baby was originally someone else's, a new positive duty of aid has nonetheless been generated for you as a direct result of that other person's shirking. It is not as if it is permissible for you to shut the door and go back to bed on account of never having consented to these additional duties.

Rather, these new moral responsibilities now obtain for you regardless, as does the experiential duress of moral decision-making accompanying these duties, all on account of the other person's failure to uphold a responsibility that was originally theirs. While the negligent parent has failed to legitimately relieve himself of moral responsibility for the child, he has succeeded in relieving himself of the present (and future) psychological duress attached to the deliberative role of caring for the child. In this sense, he has not gained freedom from actual moral responsibility as much as he has gained freedom from the proximate deliberative role.

The previous example describes a case where an agent's shirking of responsibility activates a positive duty for a third party, with whom no prior contract of shared responsibility had been previously established. In such cases, the exploited party has no specific associative duties resulting from any special relationship to the exploiter. We can imagine a different case however, where there is in fact a preestablished contract or relationship between parties and where the exploiter shirks his share of associative duties. In shirking his duties, the exploiter does not technically generate new positive duties for the exploitee as much as he exacerbates the weight and magnitude of the exploitee's presently existing moral decisions.

For instance, imagine a case of two parents raising a newborn baby together, where one day, the father chooses to suddenly walk out on the mother. In this case, since responsibility for the baby is in part the mother's, we would not think that the father's walking out activates an entirely new positive duty of care that the mother previously did not have. Rather, we would think that the mother already possessed some positive duty of care for the child prior to the father exiting. Nonetheless, even though this positive duty for the child's care already obtained for the mother, the father's exiting nonetheless makes the mother objectively worse off. Specifically, the mother is made worse off not just because she must now shoulder the additional physical, financial, and emotional demands of raising the child solo, but she is also made worse off by now being made the sole bearer of responsibility for any and all future moral decisions and dilemmas relating to raising the child. This is an important point to note here, that is, the idea that a person (or group) can be made objectively worse off by a compounding or "piling on" of moral burdens so to speak. If the originating moment of the acceptance of such burdens was from a position of pronounced vulnerability, pressure, or inadequate information, then such persons or groups arguably would have some reason for complaint.

One response to this example might be to question just how it is that the supposed exploitee in this case is actually vulnerable. While the mother, the exploitee, is not vulnerable in the typical sense (she is not economically or physically in a considerably disadvantaged position), she is nonetheless vulnerable insofar as her set of moral convictions act as a constraining factor upon her actions much like any physical or economic constraint. Indeed, this is exactly what the negligent father is counting on. The father's expectation that the mother will be a decent person and will care for the child is the very thing that allows him to believe that his parental responsibilities will be effectively picked up by someone else. The mother has now, through the father's shirking, been made to shoulder the psychological burdens associated with raising a child by herself. She is also made worse off insofar as she is saddled with the additional moral decision-making that she is now forced to exercise completely on her own in the coming years. Insofar as the father's actions have made the mother worse off in this way, he has also wronged her.

In both cases, the benefit the exploiter effectively "gains" during this exploitative exchange amounts to a sort of experiential or hedonic good, in that the negligent father has relieved himself of experiencing further psychological duress or difficulty associated with having to take part in future moral decision-making involved in caring for the child. While he has not succeeded in offloading or legitimately transferring his share of moral responsibility, he nonetheless succeeds in thrusting the psychological and experiential weight of future moral decision-making, in caring for the child, onto the mother's shoulders, thereby obligating her to sort through future difficult moral decisions that he does not want to deal with. And while he still very much bears the responsibility for the child's care, when the mother (or whoever else) is stuck wrestling with a particularly difficult moral decision pertaining to raising the child, the father will have circumvented such future psychological burdens altogether, having opted out long ago. In all likelihood, the father will be completely unaware of such future worries, having fully distanced himself from the context of actual moral decision-making.

There is something important to note here regarding our two previous examples. Unlike standard cases of exploitation, moral exploitation is not zero-sum in nature, where what should have fairly gone to the exploitee goes instead to the exploiter. Whereas in cases of standard exploitation, where what should have been gained fairly by the exploitee necessarily becomes what is unfairly gained by the exploiter, in the first type of moral exploitation, the exploitee can come to unfairly take on new moral responsibilities without the exploiter legitimately divesting himself of those responsibilities. In this way, the first type of moral exploitation here described involves not a transfer of moral responsibility but rather an unfair compounding or spreading of moral responsibility onto vulnerable agents. There is also a second, more robust type of moral exploitation, we argue, that does in fact involve a legitimate transfer of moral responsibilities from exploiter to exploitee such that the exploitee becomes the legitimate bearer of those responsibilities. Such instances of moral exploitation, we contend, often occur when the specific currency exchanged between exploiter and exploitee takes the form of not a token, one-off decision, but rather, the assumption of an ongoing *type* of deliberative role. In such cases, there will oftentimes be a diachronic rather than a synchronic relationship between the exploitative contract and the responsibilities entailed. By synchronic, we mean those cases where the contract and the responsibilities accompanying that contract obtain at the same time. This would be like our original case of Beth and Anna where Anna agrees to assume responsibility for the one-time decision of firing one of her co-workers. At the moment she agrees to the contract, she simultaneously assumes all the responsibilities associated with that one-time decision. Such a case would be roughly analogous to one-time, discrete transactional cases of exploitation outlined earlier. Contrast this case, however, with one in which Anna agrees to assume an entire new job position as the person in charge of all future firings. In this case, a diachronic or structural relationship is implied by the initial contract type and its accompanying set of moral responsibilities in that there is now a "lag time" between when the contract obtains and when the prospective and latent responsibilities entailed by that contract manifest. It is this lag time, we argue, that allows for the possibility of a full and legitimate transfer of prospective moral responsibilities from exploiter and exploitee during a morally exploitative exchange. Indeed, we see this particular type of moral exploitation most prevalently in cases involving vulnerable agents embedded within some sort of official institutional context. This latter case would then be analogous to the kind of structural exploitation previously described.

We may consider another case illustrative of this second, more robust kind of moral exploitation. Imagine that Albert is a politician up for re-election. Bob is a junior staff member who is a young, somewhat naive, go-getter eager to prove himself. Consequently, he is quick to take on assignments with little resistance. Let us also imagine that Albert is aware of this feature of Bob's character. Shortly before the election, a new board is created, designed to deal with controversial race issues in the local schools. There have been no serious problems as of yet, however, Albert believes that there is a likelihood of at least one major morally problematic issue arising between now and the election. Not wanting to have to deal with such heavy moral decision-making, and not wanting to risk getting those decisions wrong, Albert offers to give Bob a financial bonus if Bob joins the board in his place. In such a case it seems as if Albert does not unfairly transfer any additional or excessive moral responsibility onto Bob at the very moment of the initial agreement. However, there does seem to be a type of exploitation occurring nonetheless. In the this case, Albert takes unfair advantage of Bob's naivete to get him to agree to take a position that, while not possessing any additional moral responsibility at the moment of agreement, entails taking on considerable moral responsibilities in the foreseeable future. Thus, insofar as Albert leverages Bob's naivete to transfer to him prospective moral burdens that are effectively "baked in" to the original agreement, Albert morally exploits Bob in this more robust sense.[37]

As noted and as demonstrated by the these cases, instances of moral exploitation are predictably more prevalent when we find vulnerable persons within large institutional or professional structures where their negotiation power with higher-ups is significantly diminished or nonexistent given their institutional role and institutional status. Without stretching the imagination too much, we can quickly see how an unfair or disproportionate tipping of moral burdens can occur between superiors and subordinates operating within responsibility laden professions and roles such as police officers, penitentiary guards, defense attorneys, nurses, commercial surrogates, au pairs, doctors, FBI officers, and even spies. Each of these roles regularly involves high-stakes moral decision-making and therefore the presence of moral burdens and asymmetric institutional power relationships, and thus the heightened potential for an unfair or exploitative distribution of moral burdens within the institution onto vulnerable parties to occur.

The Unique Wrongness of Moral Exploitation

Given the aforementioned cases, how should we understand moral exploitation's unique wrongness? While no physical good or service has been extracted from the vulnerable parties in these scenarios, it still seems as if these agents are being wronged in some important sense. For one, we might think that these agents are being wronged insofar as their vulnerabilities are leveraged so they are pressured to experience foreseeable and excessive psychological duress,

---

[37] Note also that the phenomenon here described is substantively different from the wrong of "scapegoating" someone. In the case of scapegoating, a person is held accountable for moral responsibilities that aren't properly hers. Conversely, in the more robust case of moral exploitation here described, the moral responsibilities and concomitant blameworthiness still sit with the exploitee.

duress which necessarily accompanies the moral deliberation unfairly thrust upon them. To unfairly or unnecessarily generate for someone the psychological duress of difficult moral deliberation, we might conclude, is to wrong or harm that agent in some important way.

We may wonder however, if in cases of moral exploitation, whether agents are wronged in ways that go beyond just the imposition of psychological duress. To merely expose another person to the risk of physical or psychological harm, most philosophers would accept, constitutes a distinct wronging of that agent whether or not that harm actually eventuates. Thus, the negligent doctor who performs surgery while grossly intoxicated but miraculously pulls off the procedure successfully, while not harming his patient, still seems to wrong her. Accordingly, just as one can be wronged by being unfairly exposed to situations of physical/psychological risk and the possibility of physical/psychological harm, we argue that one can also be wronged by being overexposed to situations of high-stakes moral decision-making, moral dilemmas, and the hence, high possibility of moral failure and blameworthiness.

This arguably explains, in part, what we find so morally objectionable about the Milgram experiments of the 1960s or "hidden camera" videos that trap unwitting persons in apparent moral dilemmas. Thus, even if an agent does everything right while in these high-stakes moral situations, insofar as he is unfairly overexposed to scenarios where there was still the possibility of making a moral error (or perceived moral error), he is nonetheless wronged in an important sense. The unfairness of moral exploitation, it would seem, can therefore be located in the disproportionate distribution of moral responsibility, moral decision-making, and risk of moral failure to vulnerable agents when such responsibilities and risks could have been more equitably distributed among all agents involved, to include those who are less vulnerable and who benefit. It is therefore this phenomenon of "sticking" vulnerable parties with the lion's share of moral responsibility, moral decision-making, and risk of moral failure that is the hallmark feature of moral exploitation's unique wrongness.

As a final wrong-making feature of moral exploitation, as noted previously, we may also think that there is something uniquely wrong about unfairly and disproportionately exposing vulnerable persons to high-stakes decision-making contexts where the incurring of moral residue, or dirty hands, is foreseeable or inevitable. Insofar as moral residue ought to be equitably distributed among an entire group of agents, vulnerable agents who are pressured to be the disproportionate bearers of such moral residue seem to be wronged in an important way. Thus, by being overexposed to high-stakes moral situations where there is a likelihood of incurring moral residue, vulnerable parties are wronged by moral exploitation and uniquely so.

Admittedly, the degree of unfairness of the exploiter's gains cannot be as precisely tracked for cases of moral exploitation as it can be for standard market-based transactions since there is no "moral free-market baseline" that we can easily check against. There is no stock exchange or currency conversion rate we can look to between X number of widgets and Y units of moral responsibility. Nonetheless, this lack of precise measurement does not mean we are incapable of speaking meaningfully about excessive or unfair gains that can be captured in terms of an escape or distancing from the moral burdens described in the aforementioned examples.

To sum up and further clarify the notion of moral exploitation, consider the classic case of "Jim and the Indians" famously crafted by Bernard Williams. In the original case, Jim is on a botanical research expedition in South America when he comes upon a local militant leader and his men who are about to execute twenty innocent civilian natives (the "Indians") for the purpose of intimidating other civilians to not act up against the ruling regime. The leader determines that Jim is there by accident and explains the situation to him, but he then offers Jim the honor of killing one of the innocent prisoners as a "guest's privilege." If Jim accepts the offer and kills one of the Indians, the other innocent Indians will be let go. If he declines, then the militant leader will proceed and kill all twenty of the Indians. Now consider an expansion of this case. Call this new case Jim and His Research Crew.

Imagine Jim is on the botanical expedition, but this time, he's accompanied by his team of a dozen junior researchers. One of these junior researchers is Bob, who has just recently disclosed to Jim the serious financial stress he is currently facing and his desperation to do anything to resolve it. Just after this disclosure, Jim and his team stumble upon the militant leader and the scene with the twenty civilians from the original case. Jim and his team are given the same offer as before—one of them can choose to kill an civilian and the rest will be spared, or, if they choose not to do so, all twenty will be killed. Jim turns to Bob and asks him to make this decision (i.e., decide to kill or not kill the innocent civilian) and, in return, Jim will give him a large sum of money and solve Bob's financial distress. Bob reluctantly accepts the offer and is faced with the moral burden of making this decision on his own.

As we consider this case, remember Williams's point in offering the original version. He was not arguing that Jim should not shoot the civilian—he thought Jim should. (And, presumably, so should Bob in the second case.) Rather, Williams raised it as an objection against consequentialism because, in his view, consequentialism implied that the decision is too easy. That is, the decision to kill the civilian should be difficult and would be for any normal moral agent cast into such a harrowing situation, even if, indeed, the right choice is to kill one person to save the other nineteen. It is this difficulty that Jim unfairly thrust upon Bob in exchange for resolving his vulnerable financial situation. Jim morally exploits Bob.

Here, we see that his case clearly captures many of the relevant aspects of moral exploitation elucidated earlier. First, the experiential duress Bob undergoes in having to make the decision to shoot a civilian is in many ways similar to what a soldier may experience in war. Second, even if Bob makes the (putatively) right decision and kills one innocent, he may quite likely still carry a certain moral residue from the act after the fact, by committing a pro tanto wrong in order to achieve the all-things-considered good. Next, we would not think that Jim, by having morally exploited Bob, can plausibly claim to have entirely washed his hands of the matter. Of course, the decision itself is now Bob's to make and not Jim's. In that way, the moral deliberative burden has been effectively "transferred." And, in that sense, Jim is not responsible for Bob's choice. But, in another equally powerful sense, Jim still carries some moral responsibility for the situation because the means he removed himself from the original decision was exploitative. Again, the moral responsibility here is not zero-sum but is expanded, rather than absolved, by the exploitation.

While the cases we looked at here largely involve instances of moral exploitation during discrete transactions between individuals, just as with normal instances of exploitation, it is also important to briefly note that moral exploitation can obtain in a relational or structural form involving large-scale groups. As mentioned, it is indeed possible that there can be persistent institutional and structural elements that would render groups like commercial surrogates or junior doctors exploited in the normal sense. Similarly, we argue, such groups can be morally exploited as well by virtue of these very same institutional structures serving to pile additional moral burdens that these groups cannot reasonably refuse.

Conclusion

In this chapter we investigated some of the standard accounts of exploitation within contemporary exploitation literature. Specifically, we have looked at several major theoretical accounts and examples of exploitation, as well as investigated some of the working subcomponents of various exploitation theories to include formulations of exploitee vulnerability, exploiter benefit, social surplus, baselines, background and structural considerations, and exploitation's difference from coercion and neglect. We have also looked at the distinction between harmful exploitation and mutually beneficial exploitation as well as transactional versus relational forms of exploitation. In observing these various concepts, we have noted that the "currency" of exploitation in many contemporary exploitation accounts and examples is almost always described, explicitly or tacitly, in terms of an unfair transfer of a physical good or service between exploitee and exploiter. We have made the case here that this account of exploitation's currency is non-exhaustive and that *moral burdens* (and the distancing from such burdens) can also function as a legitimate form of exploitations' currency and, hence, a kind of benefit. In such cases, exploitees can be made objectively worse off by being pressured to shoulder excessive moral burdens and exploiters can be made objectively better off by distancing themselves from these very same burdens. We have likewise made the further claim that these moral burdens take the specific form of increased moral deliberative roles, moral risk, and moral residue. We have further claimed that moral exploitation can obtain in thin, one-off instances where moral responsibility doesn't legitimately transfer from exploiter to exploitee as well as more robust and iterative and structural instances where moral responsibility does legitimately transfer. Lastly, we have looked at moral exploitations' unique wrongness.

To be clear, we are not claiming that this idea of moral exploitation is incompatible with existing exploitation accounts; rather, this notion of moral exploitation offers us a new way of looking at exploitation and from a different starting point. Indeed, most exploitation theorists who have some minimal working notion of exploitee vulnerability and exploiter benefit (i.e., Wertheimer, Goodin, Sample, Valdman, etc.) seem fully capable of extending their conception of exploitation to account for this unique phenomenon. Hence, one of the main virtues of our account is that it puts focus on some of the subtler manifestations of exploitation that present accounts have largely ignored. So, the purpose of this view is not to pose a set of cases to serve as counterexamples and, hence, objections to these theories. Instead, our aim is to use these traditional theories to demonstrate how this as of yet undiscussed type of transaction, one of the unfair distribution of moral burdens, occurs and why it indeed counts as wrongful. The upshot of this account then is that it puts language on a species of exploitation that has gone unaddressed within contemporary exploitation literature and whose unique nature and wrongness has failed to be explicitly captured by traditional exploitation accounts.

How one ultimately cashes out the severity of and our normative response to moral exploitation will largely hinge upon more fundamental commitments pertaining to the origins and scope of positive duties; positive duties existing naturally between persons, within contracts both explicit and tacit, and among citizens within a shared social project. We will explore these moral underpinnings extensively in Chapter 3. For now, let us turn our attention away from general accounts of exploitation and our theory of moral exploitation broadly construed toward the main focus of this book— the moral exploitation of the American soldier.

2

The Moral Exploitation of Soldiers

I cannot support a mission that leads to corruption, human rights abuses, and liars. I am sullied no more.
—Suicide note of Colonel Theodore Westhusing,
June 2005, Camp Dublin, Iraq

Introduction

In Chapter 1, we explored several traditional and contemporary accounts of exploitation. As discussed, on standard exploitation accounts, an exploiter leverages a person or group's vulnerability to extract unfair or excessive benefit. This benefit is often cashed out in terms of an unfair or disproportionate transfer of some kind of physical good or service. In the opening chapter, we also outlined the concept of *moral exploitation*. On our account of moral exploitation, exploiter benefit can also take the form of a kind of unjust outsourcing or shifting of moral burdens onto vulnerable parties. As noted, such unfair shifting can be obtained in the form of a singular transaction or an ongoing relationship. Moral exploitation can occur between individuals as well as groups, even at the societal level, and can often arise in virtue of a singular contract and within persistent roles in professional institutions.

In this chapter, we will explore how this concept of moral exploitation specifically applies to the contemporary American soldier. As this book's title suggests, our claim is that many contemporary American soldiers are likely exploited in this very way. To justify this

Outsourcing Duty. Michael J. Robillard and Bradley J. Strawser, Oxford University Press. © Oxford University Press 2022. DOI: 10.1093/oso/9780190671457.003.0003

claim, however, several preliminary claims must first be established and defended. First, we must establish that contemporary soldiers are vulnerable in certain respects. This claim will no doubt seem anathema to many soldiers. As a reminder, however, our aim here is not to make the case that America's soldiers and warriors should be counted among the ranks of what appears to be contemporary society's ever-expanding victim hierarchy. Indeed, our claim here is a much subtler and more profound one; one pertaining to nothing less than the question of what constitutes shared civic responsibility, what constitutes being a soldier, and what constitutes being a citizen. How one comes down on such important issues will then establish the pivotal difference between duty and martyrdom, as well as the difference between the claim that soldiers are aggrieved victims versus the claim that soldiers have a basic duty of self-regard. Hence, in the first part of this chapter we will explain how soldiers are possibly vulnerable to exploitation and being taken advantage of in both the transactional sense and relational sense.

Next, we will briefly establish how soldiers are exploited in a standard sense and how it is that society standardly benefits from the present institutional division of labor. Many of these benefits will be obvious, but they at least warrant explicit acknowledgment. Once these preconditions of vulnerability and benefit have been established, we will expound on how soldiers are additionally morally exploited in virtue of the disproportionate amount of moral responsibility they often end up shouldering.

To establish this, however, we must answer the fundamental question: *What exactly are the moral burdens of contemporary soldiers?* This will require a brief detour into the area of just war theory and its various conceptions of the scope and content of soldier responsibility. Here, we will also look at some historical anecdotes and vignettes from America's recent wars that highlight the complicated and heterogenous landscape of contemporary soldier responsibilities; responsibilities often quite distant from the mainstream civilian sphere. From this combination of empirical data, cases, and theoretical argumentation, we will make the case that the lion's share of moral burdens and dirty hands for America's collective warfighting efforts, at least since the end of the Vietnam War, has been unfairly or disproportionately piled onto an increasingly thin sliver of the overall American population.

The Standard Exploitation of Soldiers

Vulnerability

It is our contention that the typical American military recruit is vulnerable to standard exploitation, of both the transactional and relational/structural kind, in several major respects. Again, this is not to depict the average American recruit as some kind of aggrieved victim or innocent dupe. Rather, the aim here is simply to point out how certain salient demographic factors, recruitment methods, and institutional schemes have contributed to a state of affairs within the United States over the last half century whereby the same subset of persons frequently end up being disproportionately recruited into military service relative to the rest of society who then benefit considerably and in a variety of ways. What's more, this constellation of factors means that such persons will often be making the crucial decision to join the military from a place of comparative disadvantage along a range of axes and metrics. We will now look at some of these salient features and factors.

Socioeconomics
One seemingly obvious way in which recruits are vulnerable can be explained in brute socioeconomic terms. Indeed, throughout human history, empty pockets and empty stomachs have likely played as significant a contributing role in influencing a young

person's decision to join the military as loftier notions of country, ideology, religion, or sophisticated just war principles. This is not to deny that soldiers do serve for precisely these reasons. Rather, we simply take it that economic reasons also understandably weigh heavily in such decision-making. The empirical evidence of US military members bears out this claim.[1]

A 2011 Pew survey asked post-9/11 military veterans to list the most important factors that had motivated them to join the military. Nearly 90 percent listed serving the country as an important reason for joining, and 77 percent listed educational benefits as important. Upward of 60 percent said they wanted to "see more of the world," and 57 percent said that learning skills for civilian jobs was an important factor.[2] Indeed, such data—the motivation of education, travel, and vocational benefits—speaks to the pragmatically sensible pull that these socioeconomic alternatives have on a typical recruit's decision-making. Furthermore, a 2018 Council on Foreign Relations report, for instance, noted that "most members of the military come from middle-class neighborhoods." This report further noted, "A neighborhood affluence study found that the middle three quintiles were overrepresented among enlisted recruits, while the top and bottom quintiles were underrepresented" (see Figure 2.1).[3]

Echoing a similar sentiment, a 2019 Bloomberg article, "Why You Don't Know Anybody in the Military," noted that present-day American military recruitment "draws disproportionately on the upper lower classes and the lower middle classes." And that "veterans, meanwhile, are more likely not to have graduated from high school than nonveterans, but also somewhat less likely to have

---

[1] Our work here is heavily drawn from Robillard and Strawser *Public Affairs Quarterly* 30, no. 2 (April 2016): 171–96.

[2] Again, see Robillard and Strawser, *Public Affairs Quarterly*.

[3] CRF.org Editors, "Demographics of the US Military," Council on Foreign Relations, last updated July 13, 2020, https://www.cfr.org/article/demographics-us-military.

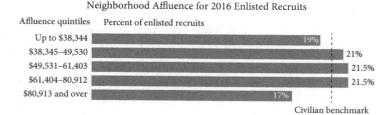

Figure 2.1

Source: CRF.org Editors, "Demographics of the US Military," Council on Foreign
Relations, last updated July 13, 2020, https://www.cfr.org/article/demographics-us-
military.

graduated from college. They are also half as likely to be below the
poverty line as nonveterans, and their median income is 42 percent
higher."[4] The article continues:

> Today, contrary to popular myth, members of the U.S. Armed
> Forces are mostly drawn from the middle class, with the lowest
> income quintile being slightly underrepresented, and the highest
> quartile being even less represented, with about 17% of en-
> listed personnel coming from the top 20% of neighborhoods by
> income.[5]

While being careful not to overstate the case, such statistical data
at least points to the influence that socioeconomic pressures have
on nudging potential recruits in certain predictable and potentially
exploitable directions. This, however, is not to be overly precious or
fall into the common cartoonish characterization of America's military preying upon the poorest and most destitute in society. Indeed,
one recent Heritage Foundation report noted that "50 percent

[4] https://www.bloomberg.com/view/articles/2017-10-20/why-you-don-t-know-
anybody-in-the-military.
[5] https://www.cna.org/pop-rep/2016/summary/summary.pdf.

of the enlisted recruits come from families in the top 40 percent of the income distribution, while only 10 percent come from the bottom 20 percent."[6] An earlier Heritage report for US Department of Defense ascensions for the years 2006 and 2007 showed a similar trend that 25 percent of the US military was represented by the uppermost economic quintile ($65,032–$246,333), with the remaining 75 percent of the military being represented by the lower four economic quintiles.[7]

While this trend is certainly a step in the right direction, it should come as no surprise that, given the events of 9/11, many American citizens in general would feel an increased desire to serve. This would then include those citizens coming from a higher socioeconomic bracket. The fact of this trend, however, still does not take away from the majority of middle- and lower-class citizens making up the military's ranks. Furthermore, such statistics fail to consider what constitutes a "living income" baseline and how relative distance from that baseline could pressure persons to join the military. Indeed, they admit as much, noting that the still disproportionate distribution of recruitment might "be a consequence of lower income individuals not having the means to get the education and testing credentials necessary to join." They conclude, however, that this statistical distribution still "overturns the idea that the military is made up of destitute people who have nowhere else to go."[8] And while we acknowledge that socioeconomic conditions are not an absolute decisive factor, we believe that economic pressures still play a significant role in influencing a young recruit's decision-making.

---

[6] https://www.heritage.org/defense/report/who-serves-the-us-military-the-demographics-enlisted-troops-and-officers.

[7] Paragraph from Robillard and Strawser, *Public Affairs Quarterly*, 2016.

[8] Andrea Asoni et al., "A Mercenary Army of the Poor? Technological Change and the Demographic Composition of the Post-9/11 U.S. Military," *Journal of Strategic Studies* 43, no. 1 (2020), 1–47.

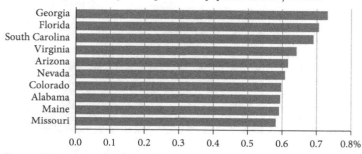

Sources: Department of Defense, CNA

Figure 2.2

Source: "Population Representation in the Military Services: Fiscal Year 2015 Summary Report," CNA report, https://www.cna.org/pop-rep/2015/summary/summary.pdf.

Region

In addition to socioeconomic considerations, another perhaps even more decisive factor contributing to present-day military recruitment and the existing civil-military division of labor is geographic region. Much like socioeconomic class, there is also a disproportionate representation of military recruits coming from key geographic regions of the country. According to one 2015 CNA study, 44.3 percent of new recruits, ages eighteen to twenty-four came from the South alone.[9] Furthermore, as reflected by a 2016 CNA report and noted in the abovementioned Bloomberg article, there are "stark regional differences in the makeup of our military, with the South contributing more than its fair share of personnel and the Northeast largely lagging behind, with a few exceptions."[10] Figures 2.2–2.5 depict this trend.

[9] Population Representation in the Military Services 2015 (cna.org).
[10] Population Representation in the Military Services 2016 (cna.org).

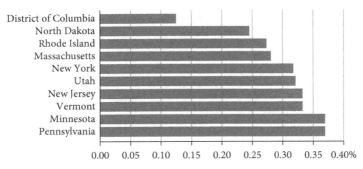

States With the Lowest Enlistment Rates

Military recruits as a percentage of 18–24 population, fiscal year 2015

Sources: Department of Defense, CNA

Figure 2.3

Source: "Population Representation in the Military Services: Fiscal Year 2015 Summary Report," CNA report, https://www.cna.org/pop-rep/2015/summary/summary.pdf.

Zooming in even closer, when we take into account the considerable number of military recruits, particularly officers, that come from high school JROTC programs, military high schools such as Valley Forge and the New Mexico Military Institute, military colleges, and military towns the comparative shouldering of warfighting burdens seems even more glaring. For instance, a 2020 *New York Times* article, "Who Signs Up to Fight: Make Up of U.S. Recruits Shows Glaring Disparity," noted:

> In 2019, Fayetteville, N.C., which is home to Fort Bragg, provided more than twice as many military enlistment contracts as Manhattan, even though Manhattan has eight times as many people. Many of the new contracts in Fayetteville were soldiers signing up for second and third enlistments.[11]

---

[11] "Who Signs Up to Fight: Make Up of U.S. Recruits Shows Glaring Disparity," *New York Times*, January 1, 2020, https://www.nytimes.com/2020/01/10/us/military-enl istment.html?auth=login-google.

FIRST-TIME ENLISTMENTS-SHARE TO CIVILIAN-SHARE
RATIOS, BY STATE, FY16

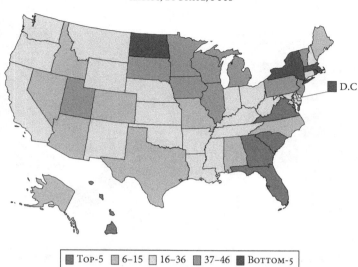

Figure 2.4

Source: Chuck Devore, "States That Defend Us—Where Do Our Military Volunteers
Call Home?," *Forbes*, February 19, 2020, https://www.forbes.com/sites/chuckdevore/
2020/02/19/states-that-defend-uswhere-do-our-military-volunteers-call-home/?sh=
11c4cac4534c.

Similarly, a *Business Insider* article, "U.S. Military Is Not
Representative of the Country," noted this same trend where the
Northeast, despite having 18 percent of potential eighteen- to
twenty-four-year-old recruits, contributed only 14 percent in terms
of overall recruitment yield.[12] Such a lopsided distribution of regional contributions to overall shared national defense should at
least prompt consideration and questions of fairness.

[12] Jeremy Bender, Andy Kiersz, and Armin Rosen, "Some States Have Much Higher
Enlistment Rates Than Others," *Business Insider*, July 20, 2014, https://www.businessinsi
der.com/us-military-is-not-representative-of-country-2014-7?r=US&IR=T.

Number of Enlisted Recruits, 2016

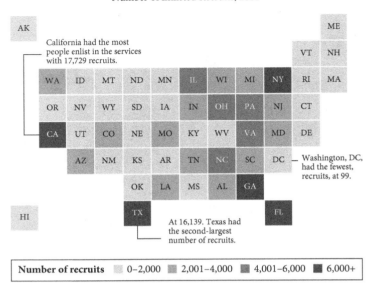

Figure 2.5
Source: "Demographics of the U.S. Military," Report from the Council on Foreign Relations, last updated July 13, 2020, https://www.cfr.org/article/demographics-us-military.

Families

Moving on, in addition to socioeconomic and regional considerations, a much lesser known factor but perhaps *the most* influential factor contributing to the makeup of America's all-volunteer force is that a significant number of military recruits come from families with a multigenerational service history. According to the aforementioned *New York Times* article:

> The main predictors are not based on class or race. Army data show service spread mostly evenly through middle-class and "downscale" groups. Youth unemployment turns out not to be the prime factor. And the racial makeup of the force is more or less in line with that of young Americans as a whole, though

African-Americans are slightly more likely to serve. Instead, the best predictor is a person's familiarity with the military.[13]

Corroborating this thesis, in a *Slate* article from 2017, journalist Amy Schafer highlights this phenomenon and likens the present civil-military division of labor in this country to that of a modern-day "warrior caste." She writes:

> In the United States, perhaps the strongest predictor of military service is having a family member who served—allowing for extended family members, it averages to about 80 percent of new recruits across the services. Going a step further, between 22 and 35 percent (depending on the service) are the child of a service member. . . . The military draws many recruits from the same communities and the same families, isolating those in uniform from society and vice versa. In essence, the self-selection dynamics have created a "warrior caste."

Shafer continues:

> About 61 percent of Americans have a familial connection to service, but only 33 percent of Americans under the age of 30 share that connection. In a government self-described as "by the people, for the people," fewer people than ever are interacting with those in uniform, and very few choose to serve. Not lost on the services themselves, 84 percent of veterans agree, "the public does not understand the problems faced by those in the military or their families."[14]

Certainly, it is unsurprising that persons growing up in particular geographic regions and/or within military families would seek

---

[13] "Who Signs Up to Fight."

[14] Amy Schafer, "The Warrior Caste: America Increasingly Relies on a Small Group of Multi-generational Military Families to Fight Its Wars. That's a Problem," *Slate*, August 2, 2017.

to emulate or embody the same general values and roles they grew up familiar with. Concerns of exploitation and fairness, however, begin to arise when the same intergenerational families end up repeatedly carrying the water, both physically and morally speaking, for the rest of the country time and time again.

Sex

Another obvious yet rarely discussed factor related to vulnerability to exploitation, particularly the relational/structural variety is that of biological sex, in specific, being biologically male in America. A 2015 report notes that for active duty forces, 84.5 percent were male, with over 90 percent of officers being male.[15] We are not the first to offer scholarly commentary on this tight historical connection between the military and masculinity. Indeed, in *War and Gender: How Gender Shapes the War System and Vice Versa,* Joshua S. Goldstein offers a thorough, cross-cultural analysis of this tight interconnectedness between men and warfare. Some of his explanations for this trend include (1) sex discrimination despite women's success as combatants, (2) gender differences in anatomy and physiology, (3) innate gender differences in group dynamics, (4) cultural construction of "tough men" and "tender women," and (5) men's sexual and economic domination of women.[16] In analyzing these competing explanatory theories, Goldstein concludes that "war is deeply rooted in the human experience, and that gendered war roles are permanent—a part of a society's readiness for the possibility of war. Males occupy the ongoing role of potential fighters, even in relative peaceful societies."[17] While we do

[15] "2015 Demographics: Profile of the Military Community," Report published by the Department of Defense (DoD), Office of the Deputy Assistant Secretary of Defense for Military Community and Family Policy (ODASD (MC&FP)), http://download.militaryonesource.mil/12038/MOS/Reports/2015-Demographics-Report.pdf.
[16] Joshua Goldstein, *War and Gender: How Gender Shapes the War System and Vice Versa* (Cambridge, UK, 2009), 404–405.
[17] Goldstein, *War and Gender*, 57.

not subscribe to any one particular theory articulated by Goldstein, we acknowledge that these factors likely do play a part in shaping young men's decision to enter the military independent of specific recruitment targeting or content. Lastly, the present US selective service requirement makes it legally mandated for only American adult males to have to sign up to be potentially drafted to war while American females enjoy no such legal requirement. While debates about changing this requirement have recently come to the fore, as things presently stand, institutionally speaking, this glaring asymmetry in institutional practice is worth explicitly noting.

Age

In our view, one of the single most significant and often overlooked vulnerable-making feature with respect to military recruitment is age. Statistically, the majority of those entering military service are recruited shortly after or during high school. For instance, a Department of Defense Personnel and Readiness report for Fiscal Year 2011 noted that, of the 283,108 applicants for active component enlistment, nearly 75 percent of applicants came from the age range of seventeen to twenty-one, with 56 percent of all applicants coming from the age range of seventeen to nineteen.[18]

The age of the typical recruit should give us good reason to think that these agents are at least somewhat vulnerable in several respects. This is not to infantilize the average soldier or recruit but to at least grant the relevance of age in morally weighty decision-making. In terms of brain maturation, formation of the prefrontal cortex, and overall cognitive development, recent findings in the area of neuroscience suggest that full cognitive maturation does not occur for the average human being until somewhere around age twenty-five.[19] Ironically enough, age twenty-five is the very

---

[18] Statistic from Robillard and Strawser, *Public Affairs Quarterly* 2016.
[19] Statistic from Robillard and Strawser, *Public Affairs Quarterly* 2016.

age when the selective service requirement for male citizens in the United States effectively ends.

Given this data, and given the average age of new recruits, one may seriously question to what degree the average recruit is capable of apprehending the full moral gravity of the contract he or she is about to enter. This includes not only future jus in bello (ethics in war) concerns that come about in fighting in war but also the jus ad bellum concerns of the wars for which they will be asked to fight.

We find it unlikely that most seventeen-year-old recruits have given such questions the moral reflection they demand before they agree to enter a job that will thrust such moral responsibility onto them. In fact, it is likely that most new recruits are not yet even fully cognitively capable of making such a choice. After all, the state itself demonstrates that it is concerned about the lack of fully mature cognitive decision-making abilities of young people, through such measures as age restrictions on everything from alcohol consumption to voting rights to legal sexual consent and marriage. These examples show that the state agrees in principle that age is a relevant factor in the ability to make valid moral choices for oneself. Indeed, it is a long-held irony of American political life that the government supposedly trusts its young people to make rational decisions about military service, with all the concomitant responsibilities and burdens that such service entails, a full three years before it trusts those same young people to make decisions regarding the consumption of alcohol. This observation gives us some reason to think age could be somewhat of a vulnerable-making factor.

Recruitment Means and Methods
Additionally, the typical military recruitment "pitch" delivered to the potential recruit is usually not a fair representation of typical service demands but instead framed in ways designed to capitalize on an often-immature understanding of patriotism, national service, and foreign policy. Further, the remainder of the typical recruitment pitch is framed in terms of incentives to be gained,

frequently in the form of future educational benefits, job skills, or calls to adventure. Concerns of exploitation begin to emerge particularly with respect to the ostensible translatability of military job training to the civilian world when one considers the high rate of unemployment or the low rate of job retention for veterans in the job market. Indeed, for many enlisted personnel, the only relevant job opportunities that make sense are jobs in policing, law enforcement, or the security sector, glutted with other competing veterans. For officers, the most relevant civilian job opportunities often turn out to a lateral move into government contractor or to another middle-management job on another leg of the iron triangle not dissimilar from their original officer job.

At present, the US Department of Defense spends approximately $370 million a year on high school military recruitment efforts, supplying roughly 3,500 public high schools with textbooks, uniforms, equipment, and so on.[20] Furthermore, the advertising funnel for military recruitment now begins not only in high schools but has also begun to be seamlessly integrated with realistic first-person shooter video games tailored for millennials and Gen Z-ers.[21] To quote Peter W. Singer, director of the 21st Century Defense Initiative, "One study found that the game had more impact on actual recruits than all other forms of Army advertising combined." Given that many people have growing ethical concerns regarding virtual and algorithmic advertising methods used to "nudge" average adult consumers toward certain push-button purchasing behaviors, the use of such "militainment" methods of recruitment on young citizens might be give some of us pause for concern.[22]

---

[20] "The Pentagon Spends $370m a Year Training American Teens," *The Economist*, March 1, 2018, https://www.economist.com/graphic-detail/2018/03/01/the-pentagon-spends-370m-a-year-training-american-teens.

[21] "'America's Army' Blurs Virtual War, 'Militainment,'" aired on *Morning Edition*, National Public Radio, March 2, 2010, https://www.npr.org/templates/story/story.php?storyId=124216122.

[22] More accurate representation of the moral risks of soldiering might not be much of a deterrent to recruits after all however. For instance, in *Jarhead*, the character Swofford relates how, when his unit was being mobilized for Operation Desert Storm, they had

Despite such efforts, in a *Military Times* article, Army Major General Malcolm Frost, former commander of the Army's Initial Military Training Command, argued that "the next existential threat we have is the inability to man our military."[23] One of the proposed solutions to this existential worry has been the proposal to *lower* the age of military recruitment to age sixteen. All other things being equal, if only this reform were to be made, however, and nothing else, then the result of such an institutional change would be nothing more than the predictable recruitment of the same regional, familial, and economic demographic but only a year younger—and a year younger in terms of their cognitive development and ability to make informed, rational moral decisions with lifelong impact.

Society at Large

A more general consideration with respect to military recruitment is the broad cultural milieu and wider social backdrop these more specific vulnerable-making features are situated against. Indeed, independent of any of these specific factors, perhaps the most powerful vulnerable-making factor of all is the increased normalization of a lopsided militarized society. From children's toys, to Hollywood blockbusters, to the military recruitment funnels that begin in adolescents' video games, to fitness videos and workouts, to sporting event spectacles, elements of an increased normalization of the military permeate the shared social fabric but in a way that is subtle and seamless.[24]

---

a marathon war-film watching session in which the jarheads cheered right through *Platoon*. Hence, in effect, Oliver Stone's antiwar intent was wholly ignored or lost on the marines, who saw it as a depiction of the glory of combat that they were looking forward to.

[23] Shane McCarthy, "Would Loering the Age of Recruitment Dix the Military's Recruiting Worries?" *Military Times*, July 10, 2019, https://www.militarytimes.com/opinion/commentary/2019/07/10/why-we-should-lower-the-age-for-recruitment-to-16/.

[24] "'America's Army' Blurs Virtual War, 'Militainment,'" https://www.npr.org/templates/story/story.php?storyId=124216122.

It is how this normalization of the military occurs we find most troubling. For it is not simply the case that young American recruits presently find themselves, say, within the city walls of Sparta under siege or within a small English town in the midst of World War I or in some Vietnamese hamlet circa 1968. In such situations, it would be fair to describe the social setting in which a young person found himself as "militarized." But something is much different with that kind of militarization as opposed to the kind of militarization presently being normalized within contemporary American society. What seems fundamentally different, and indeed so pernicious, we contend, is that the kind of normalization of war presently found within contemporary America doesn't refer to anything immediately tangible but instead to an abstraction in the forms of the so-called war on terror, the war on drugs, and so forth.

In the case of the young Spartan, young Englishman, or Vietnamese teenager, the necessity for militarization of the demos and the connection between violence and vital societal interests would have been immediately understood. What's more, these reasons and their implications would have been much more easily communicated in a tightly networked and self-correcting fashion between all members within the social community, be they man or woman, adult or child, infirmed or elderly, civilian or warrior, leader or led. Such reasons would have been relatively unmediated through various epistemic and social institutions and technological devices. In other words, the moral, epistemic, and social "division of labor" within society and the trust relationships contained therein would have been far more overlapping, networked, mutually reinforcing, and mutually self-correcting, thereby ensuring that the fidelity of the epistemic signal within the demos could be optimally preserved and, more importantly, *trusted*. Who, why, and for what reasons the demos was being militarizing would have be much more transparent. One's proximity to reasons in such cases would have been much closer and laid bare for one's own apprehension, with considerably fewer layers of institutional and technological mediation separating the representation from the Kantian "thing in itself."

At present, within the United States, the average recruit's conception of war, the military, and the reasons "why we fight," for all the abovementioned factors, seems radically different from the cases just described. Rather than possessing a representation of war and an understanding of the reasons for militarization formed through the proximate institutions of family, kin, town, village, word of mouth, and one's own immediate senses, the average recruit's representation of war could be far better described in terms of Baudrillard's notion of a *simulacrum*—a copy without an original. Indeed, given the factors discussed in this chapter, the modern American recruit's conception of both the military and war is most likely a kind of hyper-real pastiche made up of both higher order notions of God and Country blended with more primitive notions, baser gut feelings, mental images, stories, songs, Hollywood movies, yellow ribbons, and advertising slogans.

Today's young recruit likely apprehends "war" and its concomitant reasons, burdens, and consequences through some combination of the institutions of the state, the free market, and technology. Gone in epistemic saliency, it would seem, are the institutions of local community, family, and collective word of mouth, mediated now with an ever-moving kaleidoscopic lens of curated representations, algorithmic advertising nudges, social incentives, and future narratives of battlefield glory, college educations, social status, or future employability upon exit. In essence, the content of the modern-day recruitment pitch largely amounts to a piecemeal amalgamation of images and representations constituting a map referring to no real territory at all. And for the average civilian earnestly seeking to "oppose the war but support the troops," the epistemic and conceptual vantage point is likely no better.

"The Troops"

While trying to avoid overkill on this point, there is at least one final way in which American soldiers and veterans are arguably vulnerable to exploitation worth mentioning. This is to be found in the more general notion of "the troops." From slick corporate advertising, to lobbying groups, to political campaigns, "the troops," for some time now in American culture, have been repeatedly and unscrupulously appealed to in order to serve and enhance various interest groups' ends. Given that America's soldiers and veterans writ large have nothing approaching trademark or branding rights, "the troops" can often function as a kind of bottomless well for any and all special interest groups to appeal to and invoke to advance their own interests with little to no benefit ever returning to soldiers. Put another way, while civilians can say "not in my name" when it comes to withdrawing their vicarious participation in warfighting efforts, soldiers and veterans have no such recourse when it comes to withdrawing their names from use in civilian advertising or political campaign efforts.

Summary

To review, the aim here is not to give a litany of the various ways in which America's recruits are tragically vulnerable and therefore worthy of pity. Rather, this exercise is simply to show that these factors, taken both individually and jointly, can and likely do function significantly to set up one of the necessary preconditions for exploitation. Indeed, a non-exploitative state of affairs might therefore be one where recruits were nationally drawn from a more diverse regional, socioeconomic, and familial demographic, where recruitment information (and civic education generally) more accurately depicted the actual risks and burdens soldiers come to take on, and where members from society shared more equitably in warfighting responsibilities. That said, for exploitation to obtain, however, exploiter benefit must also be established. We will explore these outsourcing issues in great depth later in Chapter 5. Let us then turn now to consider this other main component of exploitation.

Societal Benefit (Standard)

As noted in Chapter 1, in addition to the notion of exploitee vulnerability, another key feature of exploitation is the corresponding notion of exploiter benefit. In this case, the chief beneficiary of the average recruit's vulnerability seems obvious: it is the remaining 99% or so of the greater civilian public. As noted, in cases of exploitation, the emergent cooperative surplus generated from the exploitative transaction, even if heterogeneous in nature, ends up being unfairly or disproportionately distributed or tipped toward the exploiter in virtue of the exploitee's vulnerability. Additionally, what makes a transaction or relationship a case of mutually beneficial exploitation versus harmful exploitation will often be indexed to the comparison class of a fair baseline and/or objective well-being baseline as opposed to the comparison class of not transacting at all.

Life Projects

The standard benefits enjoyed by wider society at the expense of a small and vulnerable populace of military recruits and professionals are rather obvious and unsurprising. One standard benefit from the present division of moral labor is the "good" of national defense and a safe civic space free of violence or invasion. This benefit is, understandably, quite hard to quantify normatively, for without it so many other major social goods are lost. Consequently, the goods here are massive, full stop. And they are enormous in normative weight both on their own and as supporting instrumental grounds for other critical goods—a point often neglected or underappreciated in the modern cocoon of relative safety that so many today blithely enjoy. Closely connected to this is the ability to plan and pursue life projects contingent upon the robustness of such a force and its continued efficacy. In other words, the good is not just a safe civic space now and for next week or next month; rather, it is a predicable long-term social space of peace, comfort, and stability whereby long-term projects can be planned for and worked toward unimpeded.

The benefit of being able to pursue one's individual life projects takes on a possibly morally problematic expression, however, when we consider the comparative downstream duties (or lack thereof) that accrue over a career or lifetime for soldiers versus civilians. Imagine, for example, that at time T-0, a seventeen-year-old recruit might act by the maxim "do your duty" while a seventeen-year-old civilian might, say, act by the maxim "follow your bliss." As time goes on and the recruit's warfighting knowledge and capacities develop, such new capacities will then tend to engender and compound more responsibilities and duties for warfighting (because who else is going to do it?), while the civilian is afforded more latitude and more opportunity for more bliss following. The effect then is often a rather stark and unfair disparity in the comparative responsibilities of duty-bearers and bliss-followers within society over time. We don't mean to overstate the case here, and we are not intending to call all civilians "bliss-followers" in some pejorative sense. But the modern miracle of long-term stable, peaceful societies for large swaths of the population who are themselves (as civilians) free from the horrors of war and thereby able to pursue their life projects is simply far too often missed as itself one of the greatest goods any and all members of a society enjoy.

Distance from Harm

A second good garnered by this exploitative relationship is a kind of absence or distancing from the battlefield and the physical and psychological costs endemic to them. Such "burdens" of war, we argue, are rather obvious and transparent to soldiers and recruits. Indeed, it's hard to imagine any recruit who enters the military unaware that such an enterprise could involve the potential loss of life, limb, or eyesight or possibly entail harsh physical or psychological hardships related to killing, dying, and breaking things. This we are not disputing. What's more, it is at least arguable that such standard burdens could, in principle, be adequately compensated for with ex post benefits in the form of monetary compensation, college educational benefits, job training, and so forth.[25] What is not so obvious, we contend, is whether the *moral* burdens associated with military service (moral risk, moral residue, dirty hands, etc.) are as readily understandable by young recruits at the time of deciding to enter the military and whether such moral burdens are the kind of thing that even *can* be distributed ex ante and compensated for ex post in a similar way.[26]

Mission Creep

A third standard benefit that has been garnered by the majority of the American civilian *demos* for the last twenty years has been the beneficial side-effects of "mission creep." As noted by Rosa Brooks in her articles, "We Have No Idea What War Is" and "How the Pentagon Became Walmart," the frequent and expanding reliance upon the American military for new, varied, and ever-growing foreign policy tasks has left the Department of Defense and its personnel overstretched in terms of overall mission (and arguably exploited).[27] Brooks captures our present state of affairs as follows :

[25] We will explore such ex post benefits arguments at some length later in the chapter. See also a discussion on this as an objection to moral exploitation in the Appendix.

[26] As noted, Michael Walzer's notion of "blocked exchanges," the idea that certain goods are, in principle, metaphysically resistant to commensurable transfer on the free market lends further credence to this notion.

[27] Rosa Brooks, "How the Pentagon Became Walmart," *FP*, August 9, 2016.

As we face novel security threats from novel quarters — emanating from nonstate terrorist networks, from cyberspace, and from the impact of poverty, genocide, or political repression, for instance —we've gotten into the habit of viewing every new threat through the lens of "war," thus asking our military to take on an ever-expanding range of nontraditional tasks. But viewing more and more threats as "war" brings more and more spheres of human activity into the ambit of the law of war, with its greater tolerance of secrecy, violence, and coercion—and its reduced protections for basic rights.

She continues:

Meanwhile, asking the military to take on more and more new tasks requires higher military budgets, forcing us to look for savings elsewhere, so we freeze or cut spending on civilian diplomacy and development programs. As budget cuts cripple civilian agencies, their capabilities dwindle, and we look to the military to pick up the slack, further expanding its role.[28]

This mission creep effect, not just in terms of specific military missions and campaigns but also in terms of the overall role, function, and telos of the military betrays the kind of relational or structural exploitation outlined in Chapter 1. In other words, an initial and earnest desire at age eighteen to defend the US Constitution, family, and homeland could, given the present institutional and contractual scheme, transform over time into a carte blanche tethering to any number of creeping, confused, and fundamentally non-defense related taskings. Those that doubt such a creep of taskings need only look at the ever-expanding set of activities that have fallen to the US military over the past several decades.

[28] Brooks, "How the Pentagon Became Walmart."

Special Operations

A final standard societal benefit, one directly connected to this phenomenon of mission creep are the benefits connected to the unique
efforts and sacrifices of the American Special Operations community in particular. Indeed, perhaps no other group has felt the strain
of the creeping-ness of the military's ever-expanding role. As a 2014
Vocativ article notes:

> The constant demand for special operations forces since 9/11—
> not only in Afghanistan and Iraq but also in Africa and Asia—has
> resulted in near constant deployments, with some operators serving
> more than 10 tours of duty in the past 12 years. The hectic deploy-
> ment schedule has taken a toll, admits the newly appointed com-
> mander of SOCOM. "SOF members are subject to no-notice recall
> and immediate deployments without clear end dates which adds
> unpredictability to the families," Gen. Joseph Votel said in written
> testimony before his Senate confirmation hearing this summer.

The article goes on:

> "Without a doubt, these guys are up to the task," says Brandon
> Webb, a former Navy SEAL and editor-in-chief of SOFREP, a
> website that covers the military and foreign policy. But in some
> places, he says, cracks are beginning to show. "If you break it
> down to the guys who are actually doing what I would call the
> 'dirty work' on the ground," as opposed to intelligence analysts
> or support staff, "what I've seen is that this particular group has
> shouldered a heavy burden."[29]

Indeed, this is a topic particularly close to our hearts as many
of these "quiet professionals" have been our friends, students,

---

[29] https://www.vocativ.com/usa/nat-sec/navy-seals-special-forces/index.html.

and comrades in arms over our respective military and academic careers. These soldiers have, in our estimation, gone well above and beyond the call of duty in their degree of sacrifice, contribution, and share of the task in America's ongoing warfighting efforts.

The costs and burdens that this thin sliver of the American population has continually taken on over the past two decades since September 11th are stark in comparison to the costs and burdens (or absence thereof) shouldered by many regular servicemembers as well as civilians. A similar case could likewise be made for pilots of unmanned aerial vehicles. Despite this stark disparity, the overwhelming bulk of these brave men and women continue to quietly and dutifully serve as the invisible seams and stitching holding the very fabric of this American project together.

Summary

Now that we have looked at some of the standard ways in which soldiers are potentially vulnerable to exploitation as well as the various ways larger society has standardly and disproportionately benefited from soldiers, let us now turn to the central thesis of this book, the notion of the moral exploitation of soldiers. To defend the idea that soldiers are not just standardly exploited but also morally exploited, we must first answer the fundamental question: *What exactly are the moral burdens of soldiers anyway?* To do this we must first take a brief detour through the conceptual landscape of just war theory.

Just War Theory and the Moral Burdens of Soldiers

Before exploring just how the moral exploitation of soldiers plays out in the real world, we must first here have a brief interlude on the tradition known as just war theory and how it carves up the conceptual space surrounding the ethics of war. Just war theory has a long history across centuries and millennia of thinkers trying to grapple with whether undertaking such a thing as war can ever be a morally justified. As we unpack the major components of just war theory, it will help shed light on what moral burdens are placed on the shoulders of warfighters. This is because just war theory gets right to the heart of the moral realities surrounding going to war and the practice of war. The best place to start is to think in terms of the *kinds* of decisions that are made in and about war.

In the simplest division, just war theory parses the moral landscape into jus ad bellum (the ethics of going to war) and jus in bello (the ethics of behavior within war). Accordingly, issues of jus ad bellum often involve macro/state-level moral considerations such as just authority, just cause, last resort, and right intention. Conversely, jus in bello often involves micro/soldier level moral considerations surrounding battlefield behavior such as necessity, proportionality, and discrimination of combatants versus noncombatants. The question as to whether the morality of ad bellum issues should permeate the moral purview of everyday soldiers generates the contemporary split between traditional and so-called revisionist just war theory camps.

The school of thought known as "revisionist just war theory" contends that a soldier can be held morally responsible for not only jus in bello moral choices but also for jus ad bellum concerns. That is, a soldier can be held morally responsible not merely for the decisions they make during war but simply for participating in an unjust war. We are sympathetic to these revisionist claims. However, if an agent's choice to become a soldier was initially derived from the kind of exploitative exchange described in this book, then, one might argue, this moral exploitation could itself form the basis for a powerful excuse of moral responsibility (both in bello and ad bellum) and resulting liability to be killed in war. From this one could argue for a kind of mutual excusal of moral responsibility arising between soldiers in war, returning us to something like a traditional "Walzerian" moral equality of combatants thesis.[30]

Before we show why this conclusion does not necessarily follow from the moral exploitation of soldiers, we first need an explanation of these background issues. Traditional just war theory, as canonized in the work of Michael Walzer, holds that soldiers on both sides of war are equally legitimate targets of attack regardless of the justice (or lack thereof) of their respective side's cause. This is due, in part, to them being considered moral equals, so long as they follow their respective jus in bello constraints on their actions in warfare, but wholly apart from any jus ad bellum considerations of the cause for which they fight. This view is commonly referred to as the "moral equality of combatants thesis" (henceforth, MEC). It contends that soldiers on both sides of a war are moral equals simply in virtue of fighting in the war, at least insofar as both are equally liable to be killed by the other. As a result, it is not properly in the soldiers' purview to consider questions of the justice of the cause for which they fight (the jus ad bellum concerns). Revisionist just war theorists, however, reject the MEC and hold that soldiers fighting for a just cause ("just soldiers") have done nothing to surrender their right to not be killed by soldiers fighting for an unjust cause ("unjust soldiers"). Consequently, in an objective sense, just soldiers are not morally liable to be killed in war, while unjust soldiers are morally liable to be killed, due to their participation on behalf of an unjust cause. Thus, according to revisionists and contra Walzerians, soldiers are morally responsible for their participation in an unjust war.

We cannot explore the various reasons for holding that unjust and just soldiers are equally liable to be killed in war without wading too deeply into the debate over the MEC. We will note, however, that many traditionalists hold to the MEC precisely because they

---

[30] Michael Walzer, *Just and Unjust Wars: A Moral Argument with Historical Illustrations* (New York, 2000).

take soldiers to be wronged in some way by their participation in war because they are used by their respective states in its decision to fight war and this is a symmetrical predicament for just and unjust soldiers alike. Indeed, Walzer himself famously emphasized the soldiers' plight in ways that may sound similar to our argument in this book. He describes this plight as follows: "These human instruments are not comrades-in-arms in the old style, members of the fellowship of warriors; they are 'poor sods just like me,' trapped in a war they didn't make. I find in them my moral equals."[31]

We have argued that exploitative transactions between the soldier and the state result in an unfair "offloading" or "outsourcing" of moral responsibility and blameworthiness from society as a whole onto a very small minority of frequently vulnerable agents. This is understood in the actual effective result of an unfair expansion of responsibility rather than an absolution of it, as described in the previous section. This general relationship between the soldier and society should not be particularly surprising to even the most casual observer of military relations. Soldiers often receive the lion's share of blame for a war's failings, even when the proper locus of blame should rest upon those who sent the soldiers to war to begin with, or at least shared by society at large. Indeed, we believe that the moral exploitation of soldiers is widespread, systemic, and pervasive in many of today's modern militaries.

If these claims are true, does this add weight to the traditional defense of the MEC? That is, does widespread moral exploitation of soldiers situate both just and unjust soldiers as moral equals, as Walzer describes, and thereby return us to a kind of tragic MEC? On a close inspection we see that, in fact, it does not. The moral exploitation of soldiers is technically neutral between traditional and revisionist schools of just war theory. We do find, however, that the revisionist view is able to offer a more complete account of the moral exploitation of soldiers insofar as it is better able to explain

---

[31] Walzer, *Just and Unjust Wars*, 34.

many commonly held moral concerns of soldiers, as we will now explain.

First, the moral exploitation of soldiers does not somehow mean that soldiers should *not* be blamed for their wrongful actions in war. As explained in the previous chapter regarding moral exploitation, just as Bob would still be morally responsible for the decision he makes in Jim and His Research Crew, so too are soldiers responsible for their own moral choices in war. Nor does moral exploitation imply that soldiers should not be blamed for even mere participation itself in unjust wars. Indeed, we hold that soldiers are morally responsible for such things once they choose to engage in them, just as in the Ann and Beth case, Beth would still bear (though unfairly) the moral responsibilities of the new job once she chose to take it on in exchange for the promotion. The presence of moral exploitation from the outset does not invalidate all acquired, downstream, or expanded moral responsibilities. If it did, note, there would *be* no moral exploitation to begin with since the basis of moral exploitation is the unfair acquisition of moral responsibility. Rather, what it does show is that soldiers can unfairly have moral responsibility rest upon their shoulders in the first place; that they are exploitatively put into situations where they then bear an unfair distribution of moral responsibility. But—to be clear—they still do, indeed, bear that responsibility thrust upon their shoulders, however unfairly they initially inherited or acquired that burden.

Hence, moral exploitation does not settle the matter over whether soldiers bear any moral responsibility for participation in an unjust war. Are soldiers morally responsible for not only jus in bello matters in war (as both revisionists and traditionalists agree they are) but also jus ad bellum matters? That question must be answered separately from issues of moral exploitation. But there are some significant ways in which the moral exploitation of soldiers bears on this larger debate. Namely, if the revisionists are right and soldiers are morally responsible for participation in an unjust cause (call this ad bellum responsibility), then the scope of moral exploitation is simply that much greater. That is, if soldiers bear ad bellum responsibility, then that burden is simply one (rather than a major) part of their moral exploitation by their state.

Conversely, if the Walzerian view is correct and soldiers do not bear ad bellum responsibility, then they are only morally exploited insofar as the burden they carry for their in bello responsibilities— a smaller range and weight of moral responsibility, though still significant. As a dialectic comment here, we don't want our argument concerning the moral exploitation of soldiers to live and die over the larger debate between revisionist just war theory and the Walzerian view. And we don't believe that it does. Whichever way the argument turns out between these competing schools simply changes the overall scope of the problem of moral exploitation.

Thus, in principle, we are happy for the moral exploitation of soldiers to be neutral on the matter of individual responsibility for ad bellum moral burdens. However, in our view, from the personal testimony of many soldiers and our own anecdotal evidence, it certainly appears that many soldiers believe they often take on unfair moral burdens in war, including the ad bellum responsibility of deciding whether to even serve in a war when they are uncertain the war is just. Any time a soldier worries about such matters they appear to take themselves to be bearing some level of ad bellum responsibility.

Of relevant note here is Nancy Sherman's work on soldiers experiencing what she terms "moral injuries" in and after warfare. In her work Sherman has chronicled many soldiers' stories of moral injuries suffered in war that track closely with the kind of harms we argue are delivered by moral exploitation. Among her many examples are several explicit instances of soldiers who have serious moral reservations and doubts about their ad bellum responsibility. We will return to the issue of moral injury at some length later in the book in Chapter 4, but we mention it here as one more data point to show that at least some soldiers do, indeed, have these ad bellum worries. Either soldiers are wrong to so worry or they are right to so worry. We think they are right to worry about ad bellum responsibility. If one agrees and holds that this burden is often unfairly or disproportionately placed upon soldiers' shoulders, then the moral exploitation of soldiers helps explain this wrong. If one disagrees, however, and holds that soldiers are wrong to worry about the justice of a war, then soldiers' moral exploitation is necessarily more limited—it is limited only to in bello responsibility.

Thus, the Walzerian view can account for the moral exploitation of soldiers but only a significantly truncated form of it. Whereas the just war revisionist can allow for the full range of moral exploitation that soldiers appear to experience. Of course, the Walzerian view could be correct, and soldiers are simply mistaken to worry about ad bellum responsibility, and thus any apparent moral exploitation on that spectrum is illusory. However, in that case it would be worth asking just what we owe to such soldiers who do worry about the justice of a war they are ordered to fight. Should society at large inform them they are wrong to so worry, along the lines of the old Tennyson poem, "theirs not to reason why, theirs but to do and die"? Better, one might think, to include the difficult questions facing soldiers who are skeptical of the justice of a war they are ordered to fight as one way they are morally exploited by their state.

Hence, revisionist just war theory appears more capable of accounting for the full range of moral exploitation that is anecdotally reported by soldiers. However, we admit that the moral exploitation of soldiers adds significant further pressure on revisionist just war theory to show how the just waging of war is even still possible given the way the real-world works. What the recognition of the moral exploitation of soldiers does for the revisionist account is to make it even harder than it already is for the conditions of genuine just war to obtain in the real world. This is not a mark against revisionist just war theory, as many have agreed that one result of the view is that the bar for fighting a just war is raised ever higher, and thus is even more unlikely to be met, than traditional just war theory demands.

We here are contending something similar for the society and the state that hopes to wage war justly. If revisionist just war theory is correct, the moral demands on individual soldiers are radically higher than the traditional view takes them to be, for those demands include ad bellum responsibility. As these demands are ratcheted up, the likelihood of just behavior occurring in the real world goes down. The same is true for the demands on a society to treat its soldiers fairly in their recruitment process and the state's just prosecution of a war. But this difficulty does not make those moral duties any less true. Even on a strong commitment to an "ought implies can" principle, just war theory reminds us that refraining from war in the first place if it cannot be waged justly is something that can (and should) be done. It is no objection to just war theory (revisionist or traditional) to argue that its high demands make fighting war justly very difficult. If what we have argued for in this book is correct, then the moral exploitation of soldiers is yet one more way it is difficult to wage a just war.

So what are the specific moral burdens for both jus in bello and jus ad bellum faced by the modern soldier? We will take each in turn. Additionally, to better understand the complexity and nuance across these kinds of burdens, we will offer both real-world cases and stories, along with some hypothetical cases that can often zero in on a particular aspect of moral exploitation and corollary burdens more effectively.

We could categorize the variety of cases and instances here reviewed across any number of conceptual buckets. There are some cases that involve both in bello and ad bellum moral burdens, while many involve concern along only one of those metrics or the other. Many of the most obvious, and likely the most common, kinds of moral burdens that will give rise to moral exploitation fall into in bello activities of warfare. Other cases exceed these boundaries and involve broader social and political issues between the soldier and the society she serves. We will briefly discuss some of those here but will return in force to this issue at length in Chapter 3. To begin, consider the following real-world cases.

Cases

In Chapter 1, we laid out our theory of moral exploitation in general. Fundamental to this theory is the notion that the "currency" of exploitation can take the form of an unfair or excessive distribution of moral burdens onto vulnerable persons or parties. As the title of both the book and this chapter suggests, our chief focus is on how soldiers in particular, because of the present-day military recruitment arrangement, might be vulnerable to taking on excessive moral burdens endemic to or associated with war. Understanding the nature, kind, and scope of what these moral burdens might possibly be with respect to soldiering has required us to take a brief detour into the conceptual space of contemporary just war theory. As we have noted, contemporary just war theory generally parses into two major camps, "traditional" versus "revisionist," each with varying metaphysical and moral starting assumptions. These conceptual and moral starting assumptions have direct bearing on what moral burdens soldiers actually take on.

Now that we have laid out some of the more fine-grained conceptual moving parts connecting just war theory and moral burdens, let us next look at a variety of cases that illuminate different features of the moral exploitation of soldiers. Later in Chapter 4, we will return to some of these cases to unpack further conceptual points and to respond to various criticisms.

Recall that our claim here isn't merely that contemporary US soldiers are excessively morally burdened as such. Rather, we are making the broader point that soldiers are excessively morally burdened as a direct consequence of a more *systemic and structural* trend within broader society that has gone under-addressed. Hence it is key that as we unpack these various real-world cases of soldier moral exploitation and moral burdens, the reader does not lose sight of the bigger explanatory picture and structural and institutional backstory as to how these persons arrived in these morally burdensome situations.

Captain Smith

Take for instance, the case of Reserve Army Captain Smith, who, as a company commander, was in charge of running a routine traffic control point in Iraq. One night, while Smith was on duty, commanding the soldiers at the traffic control point, a lone car came driving toward them at an exceptionally high speed. As per standard unit protocol and rules of engagement, Smith ordered his soldiers to flash their spotlights at the moving vehicle to get the driver's attention. The car did not decrease its speed or seem to acknowledge at all the flashing lights. Captain Smith then gave the order to one of his soldiers to fire a warning shot over the top of the vehicle. The vehicle continued to speed toward them. Smith ordered another warning shot. Still no response. With the vehicle now coming dangerously close to his soldiers and with very little time left to attempt to shoot out the tires with a precision shot, Smith made the difficult moral call, "light it up." Smith's men fired upon the moving vehicle with a hail of machine gun and rifle fire, riddling the vehicle with bullet holes, bringing it to a standstill. Smith's men then moved in to inspect the vehicle and, to their absolute horror, quickly realized that they had just shot and killed a family who were on their way to the hospital, driving quickly because the female in the car was in labor and about to give birth. For years after the tragedy, many of Smith's men suffered from clinical depression and post-traumatic stress disorder (PTSD). Smith himself exited the military and slipped into severe bouts of alcoholism and depression and two of his men later committed suicide. By all routine protocols and epistemic standards however, Smith technically made the "right" call that fateful night.[32]

The scenario experienced by Smith and his troops is as harrowing as it is tragic. Thrust into a context of such epistemic uncertainty and laden with a variety of competing moral intuitions, as well as legal and prudential imperatives, all being processed in real time, it is hard to imagine how any of us would have reacted in such a scenario. What Smith's case demonstrates is what US Marine General Charles Krulak referred to as the "3-block War"; a depiction of the modern battlespace where on one urban block a unit might be performing peacekeeping missions, on an adjacent block running policing operations, and on a third block engaging in active combat. Such a scenario, it would seem, would then require units and leaders to be able to have exceptional if not extraordinary mental and emotional nimbleness to be able to instantaneously switch cognitive frames to accurately interpret an individual as a civilian, friendly, or enemy. Given a long enough deployment window and given the increased likelihood of such predictably complex battlefield scenarios, the chances of encountering such a moral dilemma and incurring some degree of dirty hands ends up being likely if not inevitable.

Drone Pilots

Another set of moral burdens distinct to the emerging twenty-first century battle space are those shouldered by US military drone pilots.[33] According to one London-based organization, US drone strikes since 2010 have killed between 7,584 and 10,918 people in the areas of Pakistan, Afghanistan, Yemen, and Somalia, with 751 to 1,555 of those estimated as civilians. Official numbers reported

---

[32] The name of the officer in this scenario has been changed out of respect for privacy.

[33] Eyal Press, "The Wounds of the Drone Warrior," *New York Times*, 2018, https://www.nytimes.com/2018/06/13/magazine/veterans-ptsd-drone-warrior-wounds.html?hp&action=click&pgtype=Homepage&clickSource=story-heading&module=first-column-region&region=top-news&WT.nav=top-news.

by the US government are far less, estimating between 64 to 116 noncombatants collaterally killed during a similar time window. Suffice it to say that regardless of which estimates are more accurate, the emergence of killing via drone warfare has placed a new set of moral burdens on drone operators across these years.

Some of the moral burdens shouldered by drone operators are not obvious. According to an interview with one former drone operator, contrary to popular belief, interpreting the battlefield through a computer screen, rather than feeling like a detached video game, paradoxically magnifies a sense of proximity to the human target and to the immediate moral consequences of killing. According to one *New York Times* article:

> In an unpublished article, he called this phenomenon "cognitive combat intimacy," a relational attachment forged through close observation of violent events in high resolution. In one passage, he described a scenario in which an operator executed a strike that killed a "terrorist facilitator" while sparing his child. Afterward, "the child walked back to the pieces of his father and began to place the pieces back into human shape," to the horror of the operator.[34]

For other drone pilots, such moral burdens are not just restricted to in bello concerns. Take, for instance, the case of Christopher Aaron who had taken with him on his combat tour a copy of Orwell's 1984. In the pages of the famous dystopian work, the protagonist discovers Goldstein's secret book that describes

> a "continuous" war, waged by "highly trained specialists" on the "vague frontiers" of Oceania—an opaque, low-intensity conflict whose primary purpose was to siphon off resources and

---

[34] Press, "The Wounds of the Drone Warrior."

perpetuate itself. ("The object of waging a war is always to be in a better position in which to wage another war," Orwell writes.)[35]

After reading these lines, Aaron had a deep sense of dread that the perpetual war described by Orwell was exactly what the war on terror was becoming. After his time in service, Aaron suffered from reoccurring nightmares, prolonged periods of shame and grief, and a struggle with quasi-suicidal thoughts for many years.

As we see from these cases, despite the absence of any immediate physical danger, the moral burdens placed on the shoulders of drone operators can be quite severe. From in bello burdens such as adjudicating epistemic thresholds for targeting to absorbing collateral damage to shouldering ad bellum burdens having to do with possibility of contributing to a "Forever War," the twenty-first-century drone operator shoulders a set of moral burdens not obvious at the time of recruitment.[36] Complicating matters further, the number of persons ostensibly adjudicating such morally demanding scenarios has remained fixed despite the sharp increase in killing decisions and morally weighty targeting scenarios over the past several years.

> According to Lt. Col. Cameron Thurman, the number of acknowledged missile strikes   ordered by Central Command in the United States rose substantially between 2013 and mid-2017, as the size of the work force has remained unchanged. "You've got the same number of airmen doing the same number of mission hours but with a 1,000-percent increase in those life-and-death decisions, so of course their job is going to get significantly more difficult" he said. You're going to have more moral overload.[37]

[35] Nancy Sherman, *Afterwar: Healing the Moral Injuries of Our Soldiers* (New York, 2015).
[36] For more on the many moral issues raised by the advent of unmanned remote warfare see, Bradley J. Strawser, *Killing by Remote Control: The Ethics of an Unmanned Military* (Oxford, 2013)
[37] Sherman, *Afterwar,* 80.

Such lopsided piling on of moral burdens and moral decision-making onto such a thin sliver of persons not just within society but also within the military body itself should give us serious pause in considering the fairness of such a sharp division of moral labor in our societal and military institutions.

Major Hall

For another example of moral burdens, consider the case of Army Major Jeffrey Hall who experienced suicidal post-traumatic stress (PTS) as a result of an incident in Baghdad in 2003 after his unit collaterally killed several Iraqi civilians during a hit on a high-value target. After the tragic event, Hall was tasked to be the unit liaison officer in charge of giving monetary compensation to the family of the deceased; a meager $750. Upon receiving the envelope of money from Hall, the patriarch of the family angrily threw the money on the ground and demanded the return of the bodies of their loved ones (for traditional funeral rites) and official death certificates. His head hung in shame, Hall returned to his unit and began navigating his way through the byzantine network of administrative machinery to secure the bodies of the deceased along with the corresponding death certificates in hopes of salvaging some shred of dignity in this tragedy. After fighting through many layers of bureaucratic red tape for several days, Hall returned to the mourning family with the bodies of their loved ones; un-embalmed and rotten beyond recognition and with death certificates that had been erroneously marked "ENEMY" by another institutional agency.[38] Despite the incompetence of the military institution in handling this tragedy, Hall's legal orders were to nonetheless be the official bearer of these woefully inadequate token compensations; orders he dutifully carried out with both guilt and shame.

---

[38] Sherman, *Afterwar* 62–63.

It is important to note here that Major Hall's case seems importantly different from our two other cases insofar as he was not given any discretionary power. The main moral burden in this case was having to represent those with actual discretion—experiencing the worst part of wrongdoing, sorting through the aftermath, even though he had not made a mistake himself. Such a case is more similar then to someone who makes her subordinate fire a bunch of workers without giving that subordinate any discretion about who gets fired. Hall was put in a position where he had to feel guilt, shame, and more of the act even though he did not have any discretionary power as to what he was representing. Hence, we should see Major Hall's case as a subset of moral burdens insofar as he was not the bearer of a moral deliberative role but instead ended up being the human figurehead of a morally tragic bureaucratic bottleneck.

"Boy Play"
Another moral burden present on the twenty-first-century battlefield, one that seems to have failed to receive proper attention from the media and US society at large, is the practice of "bacha bazi" or "boy play" among many Afghan commanders. Indeed, rampant sexual abuse of children by Afghan commanders has been an enduring problem that many US soldiers have had to remain complicit in when working with Afghan coalition forces.

> "At night we can hear them screaming, but we're not allowed to do anything about it," wrote U.S. Marine Gregory Buckley to his father prior to being shot to death on base in 2012. "My son said that his officers told him to look the other way because it's their culture," wrote Gregory Buckley Sr.
>
> "The reason we were here is because we heard the terrible things the Taliban were doing to people, how they were taking away human rights," said Dan Quinn, a former Special Forces captain who beat up an American-backed militia commander for keeping a boy chained to his bed as a sex slave. "But we were

putting people into power who would do things that were worse than the Taliban did—that was something village elders voiced to me."[39]

Thus, instead of removing violent pedophiles and helping stop such blatant human rights abuses, the American military was actually arming and enabling such persons, often placing them in positions of greater power and authority. Indeed, for many US service personnel, the moral dissonance engendered by such scenarios must be quite severe. If one of the primary missions for US forces in Afghanistan is to defend and promote American values and human rights, then how could the tactical expression of this greater mission demand such complicity and even indirect support of what appears to be just the opposite? Indeed, many US servicemen and women would probably be hard pressed to imagine a singular act that was more contrary to what they take to be American values.

Justification for such complicity and indirect support of human rights abuses ostensibly has something to do with the all-things-considered good potentially achieved by continued US presence in the region. Still, abstract understanding of such reasons and justifications seems to do little in undoing the felt, visceral, experience of hearing screaming children being raped at night in the adjoining barracks. Furthermore, such understanding fails to undo the potential moral residue incurred by being physically proximate and yet complicit in such acts. Such scenarios, while not instances of an immediate battlefield harm or physical danger, nonetheless take a deep psychological and moral toll on soldiers and should therefore count as a kind of moral burden born by soldiers. Much like with the other scenarios here discussed, acknowledgment of such scenarios is both absent within the contemporary recruitment content and likely unable to be properly apprehended by the typical young recruit even if it were.

[39] Sherman, *Afterwar,* 147–8.

Billy Lynn

The sense of inevitability, of making a severe moral mistake, given enough time in combat is a common theme we see running throughout many of these various cases. Usually when someone is in a moral dilemma, it's because they have made some moral error earlier for which they are blameworthy, even if they have no good option now (e.g., over-commitments, or when someone has run out of time to discharge all their duties because they have been lazy or procrastinated). It seems however, that soldiers are never actively trying to put themselves into moral dilemmas or situations where they, without meaning to, wind up doing something that makes them feel guilty forever after. Soldiers often fear ending up in these situations and find themselves relatively powerless from preventing them from occurring. Indeed, something about the unique institutional design of the military (and of following orders) has an odd way of ushering soldiers to that final point of decision, often trapping them in situations, like the ones here described, that seem morally unwinnable. This feeling, even dread, of the inevitability of making a moral mistake or the eventuality of moral blameworthiness is well articulated by author Ben Fountain in his war novel *Billy Lynn's Long Halftime Walk*. Fountain writes:

> His fear up to the moment the shooting started being that of fucking up. Life in the Army is miserable that way. You fuck up, they scream at you, you fuck up some more and they scream at you some more, but overlying all the small, petty, stupid, basically foreordained fuck-ups looms the ever-present prospect of the life-fucking fuck-up, a fuck-up so profound and all-encompassing as to crush all hope of redemption.[40]

Here Fountain touches on the sense of inescapability many soldiers feel when it comes to making a moral mistake, incurring

---

[40] Ben Fountain, *Billy Lynn's Long Halftime Walk* (2012), 4.

dirty hands, or accidentally stepping on some other sort of moral landmine given enough time in combat. This perhaps might somewhat account for the strained civil-military relationship that currently exists between many returning veterans and society at large. While society as a whole might be doing a decent job recognizing the physical and psychological harms done to soldiers as a result of their combat service, they have arguably failed to adequately acknowledge or appreciate the set of moral injuries suffered by soldiers; moral injuries, incurred as a result of shouldering the additional moral burdens endemic to modern warfare.

Colonel Theodore Westhusing

A haunting instance involving a kind of overloading of moral responsibility in modern warfare is the tragic case of Colonel Theodore Westhusing. A prior philosophy and ethics professor at the United States Military Academy, Col. Westhusing deployed to Iraq in 2005 as part of "Multi-national Security Transition Command-Iraq."[41] There he was chiefly responsible for overseeing training of Iraqi police in conjunction with the private military contracting company USIS (United States Investigations Services). While on deployment, Col. Westhusing began to witness increasing evidence of deep institutional corruption in the form of fraud, gross negligence, illegal behavior, and rumors of human rights abuses and the killing of innocent civilians. His attempts to relay this information up the chain of command were largely met with apparent dismissiveness. Finding himself as the tragic inheritor of this set of moral quandaries and with no one within his chain of command he could now trust, Col. Westhusing's idealisms about the ethics of war gave out, prompting him to write the following letter:

---

[41] Robert Bruce, "I am sullied no more," *Texas Observer* (2007), https://www.texaso bserver.org/2440-i-am-sullied-no-more-faced-with-the-iraq-wars-corruption-col-ted-westhusing-chose-death-before-dishonor/.

Thanks for telling me it was a good day until I briefed you. [Redacted name]—You are only interested in your career and provide no support to your staff—no mission support and you don't care. I cannot support a mission that leads to corruption, human right abuses, and liars. I am sullied no more. I didn't volunteer to support corrupt, money grubbing contractors, nor work for commanders only interested in themselves. I came to serve honorably and feel dishonored. I trust no Iraqi. I cannot live this way. All my love to my family, my wife and my precious children. I love you and trust you only. Death before being dishonored any more. Trust is essential—I don't know who to trust anymore. Why serve when you cannot accomplish the mission, when you no longer believe in the cause, when your every effort and breath to succeed meets with lies, lack of support, and selfishness? No more. Reevaluate yourselves, commanders. You are not what you think you are and I know it. Life needs trust. Trust is no more for me here in Iraq.[42]

He then took his own life on June 5, 2005, with his US Army-issued pistol. He was age forty-four with a wife and three young children.

Sin-Eaters

As mentioned in the Introduction, much of our post-active-duty careers have been as philosophy professors teaching active-duty military officers and soldiers about military ethics and just war theory. In a recent discussion with one of our active-duty military students, the student likened the contemporary soldier's lot to that of the ancient folk concept of the "sin-eater." The story of the sin-eater goes as follows:

---

[42] Bruce, "I am sullied no more," https://www.texasobserver.org/2440-i-am-sullied-no-more-faced-with-the-iraq-wars-corruption-col-ted-westhusing-chose-death-before-dishonor/.

In the village there is one person who is treated extremely well and whose job is to eat food symbolic of people's sins so that he assumes all their sins so that they can die in a state of grace. The sin-eater is extremely old and weighed down by the sins of hundreds of people. A young man is being groomed to be a sin-eater. The old sin-eater dies, and the first task the pure and innocent young man must do is eat the sins of the sin-eater, including the lifetime of sins he has consumed that, by extension, contains the sins of all the thousands that have been absorbed by endless generations of sin-eaters. In other words, lured by the comforts provided by the adoring villagers, the young man becomes the most damnable person in history. His only hope is that one day, many years later, another young man will be similarly lured into eating all the sins that this young man will have to bear.[43]

We see this notion appear elsewhere. In the Hollywood film, *The Bourne Legacy*, for example, actor Ed Norton, playing a covert block-ops operative states something similar, saying:

We are the sin eaters. It means that we take the moral excrement we find in this equation, and we bury it down deep inside of us, so that the rest of our cause can stay pure. That is the job. We are morally indefensible and absolutely necessary.[44]

In this sense, the concept of the sin-eater tightly parallels the claims we make in this book regarding the moral exploitation of soldiers and the unfair or lopsided distribution of moral

---

[43] This concept of sin-eaters has been widely discussed across various societies and cultures; indeed, Jesus Christ is sometimes understood as a kind of archetypal sin-eater in Christian theology. Articulation of this concept can be found in the film *The Bourne Legacy* (2012) as well as "The Worst Freelance Gig in History Was Being the Village Sin Eater," Natalie Zarelli, *Atlas Obscura*, July 14, 2017, www.atlasobscura.com/articles/the-worst-paid-freelance-gig-in-history-was-being-the-village-sin-eater. The phrasing is taken from the Wikipedia entry, "Sin Eater," https://en.wikipedia.org/wiki/Sin-eater.

[44] Ed Norton (Byer), *The Bourne Legacy* (2012).

residue that contemporary American soldiers have come to take on and inherit in virtue of the present institutional civil-military scheme.

LT Robillard

While we recognize the inherent danger in generalizing too much from our own unique experiences as US military officers, it would be disingenuous to not give some acknowledgment to our own autobiographical perspectives with regard to this matter; perspectives that have helped serve as the genesis for this book and some of its core concepts.

As for myself, I entered the US Military Academy in 1998 at age seventeen with a parental waiver. However, the beginning of my recruitment began somewhere around age fifteen. Coming from a blue-collar, working-class family and looking for a decent college education, my high school guidance counsellor at the time encouraged me to apply to one of the service academies. In her words it was "a free ride" to a top-tier education in exchange for five years of military service as an officer and a gentleman. It was during the Clinton administration, and the geo-political stage was exceptionally quiet and peaceful—I thought my guidance counsellor's reasoning made good and pragmatic sense. What's more, coming from a family where my father had served in Vietnam and both grandfathers had served in World War II, I felt some obligation to continue this tradition of national service. Hence, my motivations for deciding to go the academy were admittedly some combination of a desire for a solid education coupled with what I would describe, looking back on it, as a very naive but forgivable and understandable sense of patriotism, traditional masculine heroism, and duty to country. While at the academy, I learned about the heroic acts of Alexander the Great, the Spartans at Thermopylae, World War II soldiers storming the beaches of Normandy, and James Stockdale enduring 7.5 years as a POW (prisoner of war) in Hanoi while relying on the philosophical teachings of the stoic philosopher

Epictetus to get him through. My experience in Iraq was, to a large extent, a complete inversion of these values.

Despite seeing much resistance in the larger international community regarding the US unilateral invasion of Iraq, I nonetheless ignored such objections, ultimately deferring to the epistemic authority of the commander in chief, President George W. Bush, and the experts in his administration regarding the soundness of such ad bellum justifications. Believing my chief duties as upholding my oath to the US Constitution that I swore to defend as well as to my soldiers, I opted to deploy in 2003 to Iraq despite the large social buzz of criticism.

I had also wanted to go to war to prove my metal as a man and as a warrior and to meet a worthy adversary in combat; instead, much of my missions involved breaking in the doors of Iraqi homes to snatch up suspected enemy targets in the middle of the night to the wails of screaming wives and children. Sometimes these targets were legitimate. Other times they were not. I trained at the Military Academy, Infantry School, Airborne School, Sapper School, Ranger school—all training designed for the expressed purpose of *honorably* defending home, family, and country by engaging and destroying a recognizable enemy combatant on the field of battle. Instead, I found myself in someone else's country, in someone else's private home, surrounded by their wailing family members while we snatched up their nonuniformed husbands, fathers, and brothers for reasons uncertain. This radical juxtaposition, of the battlefield with the domestic/civilian space, at times, I did not have the cognitive or emotional resources to stomach. Such scenarios seemed wholly ill-fitting to the warrior *ethos*, for the American soldier, and for America herself.

After returning home in 2004, increasing evidence surfaced suggesting that Saddam Hussein did not actually possess WMDs at all, the ostensible ad bellum justification for the invasion. Upon hearing this, I began seriously questioning what it was I had actually contributed to, where my own failures in epistemic due diligence had occurred, and where my trust in institutions had gone wrong. In consideration of my time in Iraq and the bizarre shape of ad bellum and in bello reasons I helped to realize, I would describe the military project I contributed to as neither praiseworthy nor all that efficacious toward defending the US Constitution, the American homeland, or the American people; rather, quite simply, it was *ignoble*.

LT Strawser

Still aware of the danger in generalizing too much from our individual experiences as US military officers, my story follows some similar trends we have discussed. I grew up as a military "brat"— the term puckishly embraced by those of us raised by an active-duty military parent, which near-universally involves regularly moving around the country throughout one's childhood. My father attended Officer Candidate School while my mother was pregnant with me. Consequently, that my father was an officer in the military, living around or on military bases and being a part of military communities was the norm growing up.[45]

I putatively joined the military when I was eighteen years old, when I arrived for Basic Cadet Training at the US Air Force Academy. Like Lt. Robillard, however, I had been "recruited" in some sense for nearly my entire life as part of a military family. My older brother also attended the Air Force Academy ahead of me, and I recall a time watching one of his military parades (of all things) while I was still in early high school. It was then that I consciously made the decision to follow his and my father's path. My

---

[45] My father, having a rather unorthodox story, joined the Air Force in 1979; after earning his PhD, he was recruited by the military for the burgeoning need for computer expertise. The story of my father, (ret.) Colonel Larry D. Strawser, and how he went from being a postdoctoral chemistry researcher at Vanderbilt, presumptively aiming to carve out a traditional academic career to joining the Air Force and ultimately serving for twenty-six years, is its own compelling narrative.

grandfather on my father's side was a World War II vet, and I grew up hearing stories of his war travails in the Pacific theater.

All of those familial ties surely significantly influenced my decision to join the military. I also had some very real sense that one is obliged to "serve" in some way that was bigger than oneself; albeit young, a bit naive, and not fully formed, it's true that I felt that sense of duty. There is clear signaling to a young man or woman growing up in the United States, at least in many communities, that serving in the military is a particularly noble vocation that one should be proud to embrace. For an aspiring student like myself, the service academies held a certain prestige among and kind of respect from the broader society at large. This all made sense to me and, as with Lt. Robillard, a significant advantage was that it was "all paid for." Coming from a middle-class family—like most military families, we were financially stable but never wealthy—the prospect of a high-caliber free education was very attractive for a successful student without tremendous resources.

I too anticipated a relatively calm and straightforward service in the military. However, I happened to be commissioned in the summer of 2001. I'd been on active duty for roughly a month when September 11 changed the world. Suddenly this previously peacetime force, which had not had major military operations, other than the Persian Gulf War in 1991, since the end of the Vietnam era, was now unequivocally ramping up to full-scale war. Even with 9/11 before us, however, it would have been hard to predict then that that event would send the United States tumbling into perpetual, continuous war for the next two decades (and counting).

While serving in this new military context, I came to the conclusion that I wanted to pursue an academic career over the long term.[46] But I was now faced with the very real prospect of being deployed to either of the wars in Afghanistan or Iraq. It was during

---

[46] I never planned to serve more than a few years in the military; it was a way to "launch" into college.

these years that I was gripped with a kind of existential angst—not over the prospect of serving in combat, but over the moral realities of these wars. I was proud of my service, on the one hand, and I was willing and would be proud to be deployed and fight if called upon to do so. But on the other hand, the wars themselves, and the invasion of Iraq in particular, deeply troubled me.

I had already been studying graduate work in philosophy by then and based on my rudimentary study of just war theory, I had concluded that the US military efforts in Afghanistan were justified.[47] However, from the beginning, I was dubious of the supposed justification for the war in Iraq. The arguments seemed flimsy, at best, for the official justified cause of the war, among other problems. And so through those years, a kind of dread and corollary explanatory dance filled my mind. I privately concluded that if I received orders to deploy to Afghanistan, I would, of course, go and serve to the best of my ability. But I also privately wrestled with what I would do should I receive orders to go to Iraq—a war I concluded was unjust. I would want to serve alongside my brothers and sisters in my unit, of course, and not abandon them. However, I also believed it was wrong to serve on behalf of a cause that one believes is unjust. I was wrestling with the awful decision I feared I would have to make between loyalty to my fellow military members and my integrity, should I be ordered to deploy to Iraq.[48]

As good fortune would have it, I was never deployed to either war. Alas, unlike my co-author, I never ended up serving in

---

[47] My argument was simple: al-Qaeda had committed a direct attack on the United States, and we had the sovereign right to defend ourselves from that threat. The Taliban, controlling another sovereign state, Afghanistan, refused to prosecute al-Qaeda for their crimes and, in fact, openly harbored and protected them. So I reasoned that made them morally complicit and responsible and, hence, liable targets of attack in our self-defense.

[48] The crisis of conscience I was going through in those days would today be a case study in what is known as "Selective Conscientious Objector Status." This is a new concept contending that one need not be a pacifist, as I am not, to object to serving in certain war efforts that one's concludes are unjust. There's been a tremendous amount of excellent research on this topic in recent years. See for example, David Whetham's recent work in this area.

combat; a rather random fluke of my relatively brief military service for which I am thankful to this day.[49] With those deployment possibilities never coming to fruition, the Air Force in its infinite wisdom decided instead for me to go to the Air Force Academy and teach young cadets about the ethics of war. Shortly after that time, I separated from military service, joined the DD-214 club, and began my academic career in earnest.[50] It is perhaps no surprise, given those years of wrestling with the morality of my own military service, that I have focused much of my scholarly work on exactly these issues.

Synopsis

The purpose of laying out these various soldier's cases is more than just an exercise in highlighting tragedy for tragedy's sake. Indeed, an identical exercise could arguably be performed in highlighting various tragedies that have befallen members in other communities like medicine, law, policing, and so forth. What's more, even if we constrained our inquiry to just military examples, we could likely come up with a similar set of examples and moral dilemmas experienced by soldiers within a fully conscripted military force. To be clear though, the main point of this exercise has been not just to show the moral burdens of war but also to show just how drastically the realities of these burdens diverge from the official recruitment narrative and how these burdens end up being unfairly distributed onto the shoulders of a very small minority of vulnerable agents to the benefit of the remainder of society quarantined from such duties and moral dilemmas.

---

[49] I came close three times, when initial deployment orders included my slot in the "bucket"—but each time my slot was removed after a reshuffling of the deployment package; each time for different reasons.
[50] The DD-214 is a treasured form that all veterans receive upon separation from military service.

As stated previously, we are not suggesting that young recruits have somehow been misled about the violent and harsh nature of war or are so naive as to believe that soldiering and war do not somehow involve the potential loss of life, limb, or eyesight, or the potential of killing other combatants. This we do not dispute. The scenarios we have listed here, however, are tragic *not* because a soldier lost a limb, saw a buddy get killed, or suffered some debilitating nervous system trauma. Rather, the scenarios are tragic because they are morally intractable. It would be one thing if the soldiers in these intractable moral dilemmas initially entered their military contract with an accurate representation or even a *partial* representation of such moral burdens. We find such a scenario highly unlikely. It would likewise be another thing if a fair and honest representation of such moral burdens were accurately communicated to a recruitment demographic who were then able to rationally consent to shoulder such burdens free from the vulnerable-making features of age and socioeconomic class. This too seems highly unlikely. And it would be a final thing if the remainder of civilian society was not so radically protected from exposure to such trying and sometimes debilitating moral dilemmas in virtue of these prior two institutional arrangements. Reflection on this last point leads us to consider then just how exactly the remainder of civilian society benefits from the present institutional distribution of war's moral burdens.[51]

Societal Benefit Revisited

To review, our account of moral exploitation argues that "moral burdens" unfairly taken on by an exploitee during an exploitative

---

[51] This of course presumes a broad contractualist account of political obligation; i.e., the idea that political obligations between persons within a society derive from an agreed upon social contract or agreement.

exchange can take three distinct forms: increased moral deliberative roles, increased exposure to moral risk, and increased likelihood of incurring moral residue, or dirty hands. Consequently,
on this view, the "good" technically gained or acquired by an exploiter during a morally exploitative transaction or relationship is
not a positive acquisition of any physical good or service; rather,
it is acquiring a kind of distancing, immunity, or relief from hard
moral decision-making contexts and the associated moral burdens
endemic to such contexts. What's more, we have also argued that
depending on the nature of the relationship and transaction, moral
exploitation can take on a variety of thin and thick and synchronic
or diachronic forms.

In this chapter we have also explored traditional and revisionist
just war theory accounts and have gleaned an understanding of
some of the concomitant moral burdens entailed by and associated
with each of these views. This is highly important since *the scope* of
moral burdens that soldiers come to take on during such an exploitative exchange will directly hinge on whether revisionist versus traditional just war theory is true. If the traditionalist just war account
is correct, then the moral exploitation of soldiers will necessarily be
truncated and contained exclusively to in bello concerns. In other
words, the moral deliberative roles, moral risks, and moral residue
taken on by soldiers will necessarily involve only ethical concerns
related to behavior in war and on the battlefield and will not include
moral burdens associated with the macro-level act of potentially
participating in an unjust war.

What's more, if traditional just war theory is correct, our understanding of the potential moral residue taken on by soldiers would
be directly affected. For instance, if a contractualist account of traditional just war theory is true, (i.e., if the MEC is derived from
explicit or tacit contracts between states), then the moral burdens
taken on by soldiers in a morally exploitative exchange would
be no different *in kind* from the moral burdens potentially taken
on by those in morally laden civilian roles like district attorneys,

doctors, police officers, penitentiary guards, or executioners. In the case of these morally laden civilian roles, a lopsided distribution of moral burdens onto persons acting in such roles would ostensibly be circumscribed within some sort of social contract. Hence, if the contractualist just war account is correct and an explicit or tacit contractual relationship existed between warring states, then necessary and proportionate soldier-on-soldier violence in war would not generate any moral residue since such harms to soldiers would be necessarily discounted by mutual rights waivers. The burdens on soldiers might then just admit of a phenomenal character of moral decision-making but with no accompanying moral residue.

Similarly, necessary and proportionate soldier-on-soldier violence would likewise fail to generate moral residue were it the case that the exceptionalist or rule-consequentialist account of traditional just war theory were true. On the exceptionalist view, necessary and proportionate soldier-on-soldier violence would fail to generate moral residue since both combatants would be presumed to be operating in a space where rights infringements would be conceptually impossible. On the rule-consequentialist view, the all-things-considered set of reasons for warring states to uphold a "performative" MEC, as it were, would therefore dictate that soldier rights' infringements be similarly discounted.

If the revisionist just war theory view is correct, however, then the moral exploitation of soldiers and the moral burdens potentially taken on by soldiers would be substantively different in kind from the moral burdens potentially taken on by civilian district attorneys, doctors, police officers, and so on. Again, in the case of these morally laden civilian roles, the kind of moral burdens taken on will be contained within the purview of the social contract. If the revisionist account of just war theory is true however, then the moral burdens taken on by soldiers will necessarily occur outside of any tacit contract between warring states. And since a contractual agreement internal to a political community cannot, in and of itself, generate a rights forfeiture for a combatant outside of that social contract, that is, it cannot render that opposing soldier liable, then soldiers fighting on behalf of an unjust war would be violating the rights of their opponents.

As stated previously, we are not wedded to any one version or permutation of traditionalism or revisionism just described. Were any of these versions true, however, then the abovementioned entailments would necessarily follow for our theory of the moral exploitation of soldiers. We leave it up to the reader to ultimately decide which version of just war theory is correct.

Conclusion

In this chapter, we have looked at the various ways in which soldiers and recruits are vulnerable to exploitation. While not an exhaustive list and not necessarily applicable to all recruits, we argue that many American recruits are vulnerable to exploitation in virtue of socioeconomic class, family, sex, geographic location, and age. Given this last vulnerable-making feature specifically and given related constraints due to epistemic limitations as well as neurological limitations, we believe that the majority of American recruits, at the time of recruitment, lack the requisite cognitive and epistemic resources to make a fully informed decision about the set of moral burdens entailed by military service. What's more, even if a soldier did not possess any of these age-related vulnerabilities at the initial time of recruitment, statistically speaking, he or she still likely would have been making their decision to join the military body from an exploited demographic due to socioeconomic, geographic, or familial factors. Lastly, even if vulnerabilities due to age, class, and so forth were fully absent, we contend that there is nonetheless a drastic disconnect between present-day representations of military service found in official recruitment content and the realities of the heavy moral burdens soldiers come to take on. And while improving empirical conditions having to do with recruitment content do not in and of themselves obviate these wartime moral burdens, presenting citizens with a more accurate representation of such burdens, we believe, is nonetheless a step toward greater fairness in society.

To better understand the nature and kind of moral burdens soldiers come to take on, we explored contemporary just war theory, its revisionist and traditional variants, and the normative implications entailed by each. If traditionalism is correct, then the kind and scope of moral burdens taken on by soldiers will necessarily be restricted to in bello concerns only. If revisionism is correct, then the moral burdens assumed by soldiers will be considerably weightier and will entail not only in bello burdens but also ad bellum considerations. As to the question of whether the traditionalist or revisionist just war view is correct, we leave it open to the reader to ultimately decide.

In this chapter, we also explored several real-world anecdotes and vignettes highlighting the nature and kinds of moral burdens endemic to warfare that contemporary soldiers have come to take on. From our analysis of these sometimes tragic and weighty scenarios, we see various dimensions of the moral exploitation of soldiers at play; some having to do with undertaking excessive moral risk, others having to do with shouldering excessive moral deliberative roles, and still others involving incurring moral residue, or dirty hands. And while we believe that the moral exploitation of soldiers is distinct from notions of "moral injury," the sense of a shattered moral identity, often having to do with a soldier's own moral transgressions, real or apparent, we contend that the moral exploitation of soldiers and the concomitant burdens that soldiers come to take on in war provides a plausible explanatory backstory as to how moral injury occurs for many soldiers.

We have argued that one way in which a person's life can go objectively worse is for a person to be exploited or misled so as to take on excessive moral burdens or to be excessively or too frequently placed in high-stakes moral decision-making contexts. Acknowledging that one's life can go objectively worse in this way, it would make sense that such exposure to such contexts be equitably apportioned among members of the society who all collectively benefit from having a military. This has not been the case for some time now. Rather, it has been the same general demographic and group of persons, time and again, who have been the repeated and frequent "dirty-hands-bearers" for the rest of society. The society in question is full of people who have not only benefited in ways typically imagined from this sacrifice of the few, but who have also uniquely benefited from a profound immunity from moral burdens so described.

One might wonder whether even in wholly benign socioeconomic conditions the outsourcing of duty involved in soldiering constitutes some form of exploitation that is simply inevitable. We do not rule out such inevitability on a small scale. It is likely impossible in practice to eliminate all instances of exploitation when it comes to the large-scale institutions of warfighting. However, contingently speaking, our claim is that the American society can, at least, do a much better job at mitigating the runaway lopsidedness of warfighting burdens seen over the past two decades. It is nonetheless important to note that while many theories of exploitation pertain to transactions or structural relations on the free market, the moral exploitation of soldiers differs from such cases insofar as it concerns a fundamental relationship between civilians and soldiers as mediated by the state. Accordingly, many of the intuitions we have been pumping so far have been done so in virtue of a yet unarticulated set of underlying assumptions regarding conceptions of the state and the duties of citizens. To fully understand the moral exploitation of soldiers then, we must dive deeper to consider the moral and political substructure of the state itself.

3

Soldier, Citizen, and State

We were at war while America was at the mall.
—Unnamed U.S. soldier during the U.S. invasion of Iraq

Introduction

Thus far we have laid out our argument for moral exploitation as a general concept and the moral exploitation of the American soldier specifically. As outlined in the previous chapter and as indicated by this book's title, our view presupposes a certain underpinning conception of civic duty that has been adequately satisfied by some but not by others. This is no doubt a serious charge. After all, what we claim here is that nothing less than a kind of society-wide moral failing is presently at hand in America's relationship to its military. And, in concert with that claim, we are attempting to develop a new understanding of this unique form of exploitation to better understand that relationship. First, by way of review, it is prudent to retrace the primary steps of the case. The formal moves of our argument can be summarized as follows:

1. It is a necessary all-things-considered good for just societies to have the ability to defend themselves with a military.
2. Given the nature of war, military members will incur costs and burdens. These costs and burdens include not only taking on increased physical and psychological burdens but also moral burdens (*in bello* and possibly *ad bellum*).

Outsourcing Duty. Michael J. Robillard and Bradley J. Strawser, Oxford University Press. © Oxford University Press 2022. DOI: 10.1093/oso/9780190671457.003.0004

3. Given Premise 1, someone within society must fill this vital role of national defense. Given Premise 2, persons who fill this role of national defense will likely accrue "dirty hands"/moral residue on behalf of and in defense of the shared social project.

4. Just societies therefore ought to have institutional practices that fairly distribute among the demos not only physical and psychological costs and burdens but also predictable moral costs and burdens endemic to vital roles like that of soldiering.

5. One way a just society could satisfy Premise 1 and Premise 4 is to have a conscripted military whereby all citizens equitably share in the physical, psychological, and moral burdens that come as a foreseeable side effect of collective self-defense.

6. Another way in which a society could satisfy Premise 1 and Premise 4 would be to have a volunteer military whereby a subset of persons within larger society freely volunteers to fill the societal role of soldier. This volunteer force model allows for the possibility that choosing to voluntarily bear the moral burdens of war on behalf of others may, in fact, be a supererogatory act and a basis for rightful praise.

7. Assuming a volunteer model could adequately satisfy Premise 1, we must now ask the question how this particular division of social labor could satisfy Premise 4.

8. Under an all-volunteer model, the set of warfighters and beneficiaries drastically comes apart. Given this bifurcation, one of the new emergent "benefits" enjoyed by civilians is not only an absence of exposure to the physical risks of warfighting but also a profound distancing from the high-stakes dirty hands scenarios now redistributed to the members of the all-volunteer force to exclusively bear.

9. This distancing of the broader civilian population from these costs and burdens endemic to war has led to a further distancing from the big picture moral questions surrounding the decisions to go to war in the first place. That is, both the *in bello* and many of the *ad bellum* moral responsibilities and

duties of war have been shifted away from the whole and onto these select few.

10. We therefore argue that the present American societal and state arrangement fails to satisfy Premise 4. It fails on account of the morally exploitative elements of the present-day military recruitment system ex ante; the nature and kind of compensation ex post; and a latent, dysfunctional, and ongoing morally exploitative relationship between society and soldiers as a whole.

This view helps explain and understand a variety of specific practices. For example, that average recruits, for reasons of socioeconomic pressures, familial, regional, and age-related vulnerabilities, and exploitative and/or misleading recruitment practices, are often compelled to unfairly take on moral burdens and moral costs endemic to warfare that they would not have rationally agreed to take on at the time of recruitment. What's more, in terms of ex post compensation, the *kind* of compensation soldiers receive on account of this initially exploitative interaction is fundamentally inapt and incommensurable given the kind of moral burdens exploited recruits frequently incur. That is, monetary benefits, education, job skills training, or social niceties might be out of sync with the moral realities of what it means to be a soldier. And, finally, the lack of shared moral ownership of the decision by the state and society to go to war further contributes to the radical, moral disconnect between the average civilian citizen and the individual soldier who must live out those collective decisions. In some very real sense, that individual soldier ends up—unfairly and wrongly—holding the bag of excessive moral responsibility for, as well as participation in, the wars his society collectively chooses to wage. The concept of the moral exploitation of soldiers is therefore parasitic upon a wider conception of duty to country, one in which some persons within society (soldiers) have satisfied that duty— some many times over—while a majority of others within society have not satisfied that duty at all, often to their benefit. While we are not arguing here that *all* citizens have a duty to serve in the military or in a strict martial capacity per se, (positive) duty to one's country, we nonetheless assert, is not exhausted by merely paying taxes, attending jury duty, and, for men (at present) signing up for selective service at age eighteen. Otherwise, if it were, then our language of an "outsourcing" of some kind of duty would, by necessity, not be tracking anything. Hence, on our view, the duties of citizenship entail some thicker set of moral commitments that are, at present, being disproportionately or unfairly distributed amongst the shared political collective.

So what exactly does one owe to one's country? And, further, what constitutes going beyond that call of duty? It is this later question we will end up exploring at length in this chapter because we find taking on the moral risks of military service can itself be a kind of above-and-beyond moral act.

Conceptions of Duty to Country

As noted at the end of Chapter 2, while most theories of exploitation concern transactions and activities in the free market, our account of the moral exploitation of soldiers is distinct insofar as it concerns exploitation of citizens not by a free-market entity but by the state itself. Baked into this view of the moral exploitation of soldiers is therefore a tacit set of assumptions as to what duties citizens have to one another and to the country, and, importantly, what reciprocal duties the country has (via the state) to its citizens.[1] This point is crucial since among the reasons appealed to in the original recruitment pitch to get citizens to join the military is an explicit

---

[1] Importantly, we assume here that "the country" and the state/government is not identical to a nation, its constitution, and its people. However, we are assuming here that in a just, virtuous, and well-functioning society, the state functions as a just proxy whereby citizens' collective duties to one another can be best coordinated and discharged.

appeal to duty to country. It might then behoove us to briefly consider the moral assumptions underpinning such an appeal.

Throughout human history, philosophers have posited all kinds of conceptions of the state and societal coordination and thereby, explicitly or implicitly, duty to country. From robust conceptions of the state envisioned in Plato's *Republic* or Hobbes's *Leviathan,* to Aristotelean and Christian conceptions of monarchism, aristocracy, and republicanism, to Kantian conceptions of cosmopolitanism, to Nozickian and anarcho-capitalist conceptions of a completely stateless society, philosophers have offered many broad-ranging theories as to what human social organization ought to best look like as well as what rights and duties attach to such conceptions. Our aim here is not to give a fully worked out theory of nationalist versus cosmopolitan versus anarchist conceptions of political world ordering. Indeed, a fair and thorough treatment of this topic would warrant a book of its own. Suffice it to say, we reject the two poles of total anarchism and total cosmopolitanism. In other words, we reject the notion that one has *no duties whatsoever* to one's own country (intrinsically or instrumentally) and the notion that one's cosmopolitan duties to the world at large swamp one's particular duties to country entirely thereby warranting a complete dissolution of national partiality or the nation-state as such. Yet we also reject the notion that partiality to nation should trump any and all other extra-national moral duties (such as intervening to stop genocide, for instance, and many others) in all circumstances.

The moral underpinnings of duty to country, we argue, derives from a variety of sources. Generally speaking, we make the assumption that duty to county derives, at least partially, from a broadly contractualist foundation; that is, the assumption that autonomous persons within a shared social contract or set of social agreements can make legitimate positive and negative rights claims upon one another in virtue of that shared contract. Following Locke, a citizen's special duty to nation arguably derives from some form of explicit contract, like swearing allegiance to a constitution or in the form of a tacit contract. With respect to the latter, if one regularly participates in a given political project and reaps the many goods and benefits of that project over a long enough length of time, then, even if one does not explicitly announce entering a social contract with other members of that political project, assuming that political project is minimally just, their continued presence, participation, and reaping benefits in that project nonetheless constitutes assenting to a tacit contract of sorts. This then gives some plausible moral grounding, if only partially, for a positive duty of citizenship to entail military service for the purposes of just national defense.

Next, we likewise assume that a citizen's duty to country derives partially from an inheritance or stewardship relationship that present citizens share with the collective social project as they pass that social project and its accrued goods onto posterity. To quote Burke:

> You will observe, that from the *Magna Carta* to the Declaration of Rights, it has been the uniform policy of our constitution to claim and assert our liberties, as an entailed inheritance derived from us from our forefathers, and to be transmitted to our posterity; as an estate specially belonging to the people of this kingdom without any reference whatever to any other more general or prior right.[2]

Taken in conjunction, we argue that for these contractualist and inheritance-based reasons, citizens within a minimally just society have a general prima facie duty to country. If one therefore accepts the notion that one's country is a good that ought to be sustained, then the question raised is how the sustainment of that good is to be pragmatically realized. Such sustainment necessarily leads us to the particular question of how the shared good of a nation is to be defended. It is our further claim here that the sustainment of the nation, its institutions, its infrastructure, its free markets, its internal

---

[2] Edmund Burke, *Reflections on the Revolution in France.*(Oxford, 2009), 37.

governance, its domestic sphere, its art, culture, and way of civic life is contingent upon and parasitic upon the ongoing success of its defense and hence the success of those persons who defend that perimeter. To quote Richard Grenier, who was paraphrasing Orwell, "We sleep soundly in our beds, because rough men stand ready in the night to do violence on those who would harm us."[3]

Thus, despite the vital importance of the values of the domestic sphere for both individual and group flourishing, such values are not in and of themselves self-sustaining on their own accord. In other words, the values of the domestic sphere, of civil and peaceful order, of civilized governance, of free-market exchange, and so many more are only realizable and sustainable provided more robust moral and ontological preconditions allowing for such values to emerge in the first place necessarily involve the threat of and possible use of force and violence. This brute fact is one that many in our modern era prefer not to dwell on—or even accept. Yet it holds true whether one believes that one's moral and political commitments terminate at the level of the nation or extend beyond one's national borders partially or completely. Nation-states still need armies for national defense. United Nations coalitions still need soldiers for peacekeeping and humanitarian missions. And a cosmopolitan world government would still need some set of willing bodies to fulfill the role of a world police force. Accordingly, regardless if one believes that morality warrants a more Westphalian nation-state model of political world ordering or if morality warrants a more cosmopolitan orientation, there is no escaping the necessity of some to serve in a military capacity. Further, it has nonetheless *contingently* been the case that for the last half century, the lion's share

---

[3] This quote is commonly attributed to Orwell, but Grenier actually coined it, as a way of paraphrasing what he took Orwell to be arguing for across many works. Richard Grenier, "Perils of Passive Sex," *Washington Times,* April 6, 1993. After this original quote from Grenier, the line has been subsequently misattributed to Orwell in multiple places.

of collective American foreign policy decisions, as well as their concomitant moral burdens, have been shouldered by the same 1% of American citizens. Hence, whether political obligations extend minimally, considerably, or not at all beyond the scope of one's own national borders, it has nonetheless been the case that the same small sliver of American society has been the one exclusively shouldering and discharging these political duties for a very long time.

This returns us to the central question animating this book: Given that someone *must*, who amongst the group *ought* to fight and defend?

One obvious answer to this question would be to simply fill such a social role based upon features of capacity and temperament. In other words, some subsection of persons within a given social project (often fighting-aged young men) will tend to have a natural capacity and psychological predisposition toward things like aggression, risk-taking, violence, hardship, stoicism, and self-sacrifice. Accordingly, absent a situation of imminent existential threat, a practical division of labor would be to have some subsection of a given demos fulfill the role of soldier while other subsections fulfill other vital and heterogenous domestic roles (e.g., parents, judges, doctors, clergy, educators, artisans, and countless others) within the overall social project all necessary for its total flourishing.

Such a division of labor, however, still seems in conceptual tension with the American ideal of the "individual pursuit of happiness." Within contemporary society, there is a tacit sentiment that it would certainly be nice for society if there were educators, doctors, parents, carpenters, and the rest. But at present, we find no corresponding explicit appeal to a civic duty for the fulfillment of such roles as we do with the armed forces. We see no such similar appeals to young citizens to become doctors or teachers explicitly for reasons of a robust duty to nation.[4] As previously noted, beyond the

---

[4] Though, we note, perhaps this is changing. The "Teach for America" program could be seen as an embryonic effort at making "service to country" appeals for the teaching

positive duties of paying taxes, attending jury duty, and, for men exclusively, signing up for selective service at the age of eighteen, the average citizen in America can consider *all* of his or her positive duties to country to be completely and totally fulfilled.

Given the exploitative elements of present-day military recruitment, however, and given the compounding of duties and moral responsibilities over time associated with military service, such a state of affairs arguably generates the kind of pernicious normative caste system previously noted, one between duty bearers and bliss followers. In other words, those who initially respond to an ostensible call of duty to serve will thereafter be duty bound and considerably so, and those who don't initially respond to the call of duty will thereafter have no corresponding civic duties whatsoever beyond the very minimal set of duties previously mentioned. But is this right? Is this the best structural and institutional arrangement for societal civic duties to be apportioned? Is it the case that those citizens who did not respond to a duty to serve at age eighteen have no other positive duties to their fellow citizens and to the shared social project thereafter? Not even, say, duties of an epistemic sort? This last point regarding epistemic duties of citizens, perhaps cuts to the heart of what it is that we find so problematic about the present division of moral labor in the country between civilians and soldiers.[5] Given the present-day institutional division of labor between the military body and the civilian principle, the military derives its warfighting responsibilities and duties, at least in part, from the will of the civilian demos generally and from the civilian representatives of the demos officially. The duties of the military are therefore conditional on the corresponding epistemic responsibilities presumably held up by a vigilante civilian principle.

---

profession. But such instances are fleeting and unorthodox and presently infinitesimal compared with such appeals made for military service.

[5] Such epistemic duties might involve something like a duty to vote for instance.

In, "Democratic Duty and the Moral Dilemmas of Soldiers," Cheyney Ryan notes the moral problems that arise within society when this division of labor pertaining to warfighting responsibilities drifts too far apart. Ryan writes:

> The key empirical assumption is that a democratic government will generally go to war for legitimate reasons; more specifically, it will generally go to war for reasons of self-defense.... A key element in these views is the link between those who decide about war and those who must be bear the bodily and financial costs of war, then the citizenry generally will make the decision prudently, and generally opt for war only in cases of self-defense.[6]

The "link" that Ryan notes, between decision-makers and decision-bearers with respect to America's ongoing war efforts over the past two decades has arguably become lost. Hence, whether it be Bush administration epistemic negligence with respect to WMDs (weapons of mass destruction) in Iraq, Obama-era non-transparency with respect to targeted killing operations, or just a general civilian apathy for the near two decades worth of ongoing Middle Eastern warfighting, a reasonable case can be made that the civilian principle (both officially in the form of governmental bodies and unofficially in terms of general society) has failed in upholding this corresponding conditional duty of epistemic due diligence while soldiers have nonetheless upheld *their* corresponding duty to be employed to fight. Soldiers therefore, we argue, have some reasonable grounds for complaint that is far from whining. Indeed, the grounds for complaint aren't merely an issue with the shouldering of warfighting duties. Rather, grounds for complaint involve a failing of the epistemic division of labor on the part of civilians while such warfighting duties are nonetheless

---

[6] Cheyney Ryan, "Democratic Duty and the Moral Dilemmas of Soldiers," *Ethics* 122, no. 1 (2011), 10–42, 2.

shouldered. Put simply, in deciding to fulfill their duty to country in the particular form of military service, a soldier's decision to join does not thereby *absolve* the remaining 99% of the country—be it in the organs of government or writ large within greater society—of their corresponding epistemic duties to make sure that their fellow countrymen are employed wisely and justly.[7]

If we regard the state as an instrumental proxy for coordinating the negative and positive duties shared among citizens, then how that instrumental proxy apportions tasks and duties amongst its citizens matters significantly in terms of justness, fairness, and proportionality. The state therefore arguably has a duty not to exploit one particular, small segment of its overall population in order to fulfill its task of apportioning such tasks and duties.

Supererogation and Moral Exploitation

Regarding the division of moral labor between citizens, there is a further point yet to be explored. Namely, it is the issue of supererogation and how military service to one's country may or may not fit the bill. Supererogation, or supererogatory acts, involve what one would consider "going above and beyond the call of duty," or, literally in the Latin, "to pay out more than what one is due." Medal of Honor winners, giving to charity, Mother Theresa, sacrificing oneself for another, Clara Barton, Mahatma Gandhi, and so on are the kinds of examples often thought of as typical supererogatory acts and actors. Given the moral space of the supererogatory then, two possible interpretations arise with respect to our notion of the moral exploitation of soldiers. Specifically, one might ask, are we talking about an exploitative scenario whereby one party fails

---

[7] We are therefore open to the possibility that conditions in civil-military relations could get so lopsided with respect to shouldering *in bello* and *ad bellum* responsibilities that soldiers would be permitted or even obligated to opt out via some form of conscientious objection.

to satisfy the minimum standard of a *shared* duty, thereby unfairly leaving the other party to carry more than his or her fair share of the moral responsibility? Or are we talking about a scenario whereby one party doesn't satisfy a certain duty on account of another party willfully choosing to shoulder *more* than his or her fair share? With respect to this latter case, if someone in society wants to go beyond the call of duty and shoulder more than his or her fair share of the moral load with respect to national defense, then why can't we then say that the other party is in fact absolved of their duty and that no exploitation is actually taking place? Put another way, does supererogation—if it is occurring—conceptually cancel out the possibility of exploitation?

Before we can answer this question adequately, we must further unpack the morally peculiar kind of supererogation that seems to be unique (or at least especially rare) to the case of military service. Indeed, in standard supererogation cases, like that of charitable giving or organ donation, the act in question is presumed to be prima facie morally permissible and absent of any kind of intrinsic wrongness or harmfulness. Conversely, with respect to military service, the "good" of the soldier's act to serve is, in part, precisely constituted by a voluntary taking on of additional risk of (potentially) doing something wrong for the sake of the group.[8]

As we have argued, the risks that citizens take on when they choose to join the military are not exhausted by mere physical risks to life or limb. Indeed, there is another kind of risk that individuals incur when they serve. Namely, they take on moral risks, which are both numerous and weighty. These moral risks include the likes of failing to serve honorably in the grim tasks of waging war

---

[8] One may worry how it is possible to even talk about supererogation (going "above and beyond") if there is also a larger "duty" to serve. The answer lies in the nature of supererogatory acts themselves. The short answer is that some duties cannot be subdivided but must be undertaken by an individual; they are free floating, in some sense, and need to be taken on by some moral actor, but not any particular actor. See later in the chapter for a deeper discussion of supererogation.

itself—perhaps failing to make a correct split-second decision over life-or-death stakes under extreme epistemic uncertainty and duress. But it also includes the moral risk that individuals could be misused more generally, as instruments of the state they serve by being commanded to fight in an unjust war. Individuals choose to become soldiers for a wide range of motivations, be it a genuine desire to selflessly serve one's country, perhaps for the financial incentives military service can garner, or a multitude of other, perfectly legitimate, reasons. Yet, as Jeff McMahan has written, "Whatever their motivation, they are committing themselves to become weapons controlled by others whose purposes cannot be reliably predicted."[9]

Taking this moral risk as a starting point, some have asked if it is morally permissible (much less prudential or wise) for individuals to knowingly take on the potentially extreme moral risk of military service. For many it will seem obvious that one should *not* willingly take on the kinds of risks just discussed if they can possibly help it.[10] But what if we, collectively, need someone to take on those risks? Including taking on the specific moral risk that we, collectively, may morally fail in sending that person to wage an unjust war. In that case, one might plausibly conclude that the willful assumption of such moral risk is, in fact, a morally praiseworthy act—one that goes above and beyond the call of duty.

The rough-and-ready argument for this kind of view runs as follows. First, begin with the premise that in the contemporary world a state military is a necessary—and thereby morally justified—institution for at least some modern liberal democracies. Second, given that it is necessary and justified, it follows that it will

[9] Jeff McMahan, "The Moral Responsibility of Volunteer Soldiers: Should They Say No to Fighting in an Unjust War?," *Boston Review*, November 2013, http://bostonreview.net/forum/jeff-mcmahan-moral-responsibility-volunteer-soldiers.

[10] As veterans ourselves, we have been surprised how widespread this view is—the surprise or confusion by many as to *why* one would intentionally take on such moral burdens or risks—especially among those who have never served, of course.

be necessary and justified for some subset of individuals within such a society to serve in the military. But this entails that it will be necessary for some individuals to take on the moral risks of military service—including the particular moral risk that they may end up doing wrong by actively participating in an unjust war that their nation wages. As such, given that society needs some subset of its number to assume this risk, it can arguably be a supererogatory act for an individual to voluntarily do so and willingly bear the burden of this moral risk on behalf of the many.[11] These individuals carry out a noble, selfless act in their willingness to volunteer and shoulder such moral risk so that the rest of us do not have to, and, for that, their voluntary service should be rightfully morally praised as going "above and beyond."[12] Call this the *Noble Risk Argument* for voluntary military service. Right away, we see that this argument has some counterintuitive features. One looming puzzle, as previously noted, is that if this reasoning is correct, then those individuals do *right*, in part, by agreeing to take on the risk of doing *wrong*.

Some here may think this argument doesn't even get out of the gate, however, because of objections to the notion of "taking on"

---

[11] This line of reasoning is making an important assumption about these incurred risks. Namely, the moral risk here incurred is that they may fight in an unjust war. However, in a functioning democracy, one could argue that the rest of the population similarly bears the risk of being responsible for ordering those soldiers to fight in an unjust war. We're here assuming there is a relevant difference on the extent to which these moral risks should be weighed and the greater moral risk is actually fighting in an unjust war, bringing with it the risk of oneself being the person who kills non-liable people. (Thanks to Helen Frowe for this point.)

[12] Similar to the previous note, here again we must clarify. (Thanks again to Helen Frowe.) One might worry this formulation assumes a rather narrow view of the moral responsibility we all hold for our respective countries going to war, but that is mistaken. On our view, we all (combatants and noncombatants alike) risk *causing* unjust killings in war (be it by voting for a government that choses to wage war, by paying taxes to support that war effort, or some other contribution, and so on); whereas some subset of the population (combatants) risk being the ones inflicting those wrongful killings. It's an important point that we cannot resolve here. But the Noble Risk Argument presumes that there is a nontrivial, relevant difference in the moral weight of these risks (i.e., it's morally worse to be the person who actually does the killing, rather than one of millions of people sharing in a distributed decision).

moral risks (or moral responsibility and so on) on behalf of others. This is complex, but to give some intuitive appeal to the basic concept, consider a dilemma the characters come across in Margaret Atwood's *The Handmaid's Tale*. The characters are attempting a life-and-death stakes escape and realize, tragically, that their cat creates a problem.[13]

> The cat, is what he said.
> Cat? I said, against the wool of his sweater.
> We can't just leave her here.
> I hadn't thought about the cat. Neither of us had.
> Our decision had been sudden, and then there had been the planning to do.
> I must have thought she was coming with us.
> But she couldn't, you don't take a cat on a day trip across the border.
> Why not outside? I said. We could just leave her.
> She'd hang around and mew at the door. Someone would notice we were gone.
> We could give her away, I said. One of the neighbors.
> Even as I said this, I saw how foolish that would be.
> I'll take care of it, Luke said.
> And because he said it instead of her, I knew he meant kill.
> That is what you have to do before you kill, I thought.
> You have to create an it, where none was before . . .
>
> Luke found the cat, who was hiding under our bed. They always know. He went into the garage with her. I don't know what he did, and I never asked him. I sat in the living room, hands folded in my lap. I should have gone out with him, taken that small responsibility. I should at least have asked him about it afterwards, so

---

[13] We are indebted to Casey Johnson for this example.

he didn't have to carry it alone; because that little sacrifice, that snuffing out of love, was done for my sake as well.[14]

Presume that killing the cat was a justified, perhaps even necessary, albeit tragic act, all things considered for the characters in that scenario. It is this notion of Luke taking on "that small responsibility" on her behalf that is operative here. If we want to make the parallels to the Noble Risk Argument even stronger, we could presume that there's a moral risk they are making the wrong decision. In which case Luke is taking on that risk, in a different way than she is, by being the one to carry out the deed is in some sense a noble shielding of her (at least partially) from the acts of that moral risk. The analogy is imperfect on several fronts because the act does not include the kind of "big picture" moral risk required for the Noble Risk Argument. Further, one might think this is simply a kind of taking on a dirty hands problem on behalf of another, but that misses the mark as well. What the story does show, is this simple first step of the idea of some moral act being done "for my sake as well" by the other. Someone had to take on this necessary, grim task; it was noble that Luke did it so she could be spared, not only from the trauma itself but in some sense (at least partially) from the moral trauma as well.

It is worth stressing at the outset that something like this kind of moral reasoning is regularly voiced by military members serving today, which is precisely why we find it worthy of careful philosophical exploration. Perhaps it will come as a surprise to some readers, but many individual soldiers are keenly aware of not only the physical but also the *moral* risks their military service entails.[15]

---

[14] Margaret Atwood, *The Handmaid's Tale* (Boston, 2017), 192–193.

[15] For anecdotal evidence of this, I (Bradley) offer my own experience educating hundreds, if not thousands, of military members over the past decade, including members across all ranks and services, as well as from dozens of different countries. I have heard various versions of this Noble Risk Argument presented explicitly while teaching ethics at the Naval Postgraduate School. Of note is that, anecdotally, the prevalence of this argument has seemed to grow in recent years.

Many then view their own service as a kind of self-sacrificial assumption of those risks for the good of the rest of society. Accordingly, this creates a puzzle for the view we argue for in this book. If we regard the voluntary shouldering of additional and necessary moral risks for the sake of the group to be not only morally permissible but, indeed, sometimes also supererogatory and therefore praiseworthy, then a conceptual tension arises for our original claims regarding the moral exploitation, and hence wronging, of soldiers. This tension can be expressed in the two following competing propositions:

1. The voluntary taking on of necessary moral risks for the sake of the group is supererogatory and therefore worthy of praise.
2. Those who have voluntarily taken on necessary moral risks for the sake of the group have somehow been exploited and wronged by that group and therefore warrant some kind of compensation or additional recognition and respect.

On its face, these competing claims seem to be contradictory. For instance, consider the case of the person who, in the middle of the night during a snowstorm, voluntarily decides to shovel an extra path in the street in front of his neighbor's driveway so that his neighbor's car can get out in the morning. Suppose also that he does this without his neighbor's awareness. On most accounts, most people would regard this person's actions to have been at least permissible if not supererogatory. That being said, most people would also reject the idea that the snow-shoveler could then justifiably demand monetary compensation from his neighbor for his random act of kindness where no voluntary contract was ever initially agreed upon. Furthermore, most people would not think that the snow-shoveler would count as being wronged or exploited were the neighbor to refuse to compensate him. Under most supererogation cases, we do not therefore think that a supererogatory actor has any grounds to demand ex post compensation.

The solution to this paradox, we argue, can be located in the one-off transaction versus ongoing relationship distinction outlined earlier in Chapters 1 and 2. In granting this distinction, we contend that it is indeed conceptually possible to regard the taking on of additional moral risk of doing something wrong for the sake of the group to be at once supererogatory but also potentially morally exploitative. This is so if we consider the possibility that an initially supererogatory one-off act or agreement or even mere intention can become a morally exploitative relationship over a length of time or a changing set of circumstances.

Consider the case of a family member who agrees to take on the sole task within the family of caring for a dying grandmother's terrier puppy only to later realize that it is a fast-growing Great Dane. Despite the initial supererogatory act of agreeing to shoulder the responsibility of raising the dog solo, the compounding of emergent risks and responsibilities baked into the original agreement eventually show themselves to exceed the reasonable scope of capacities of the original actor thereby giving him some justifiable grounds for complaint or renegotiation. If the rest of the family members, in light of this new information still refused to lend a hand with raising the dog, all while still garnering the added benefit of necessary physical protection offered by the beast, then, arguably, the sole family member could justifiably claim to be morally exploited by the rest of the family. At the same time, however, we could still regard the family member as doing something supererogatory and morally praiseworthy in his initial agreement to take responsibility for the dog.

Accordingly, we can see how initially fair agreements, as well as initially supererogatory actions for the sake of the group, over time, can sometimes transform into a kind of ongoing relationship whereby the state of affairs can be said to have become morally exploitative, unfair, or pernicious in terms of respective responsibilities and benefits distributed amongst the participants. In such cases, claims of moral exploitation and demands for renegotiation or compensation are justified while still maintaining the original praiseworthiness of the initial decision to shoulder such burdens.

We argue that it is at least contingently the case that since the end of the Vietnam War—and certainly over the last two decades' worth of continuous American warfighting—that just such an ongoing morally exploitative relationship between the 99% and the 1% within American society has set in. Furthermore, such an ongoing relationship, we contend, has set in despite the initial supererogatory nature of the 1%'s initial agreement to serve.

This, of course, is assuming that the initial contract and agreement in question was arrived under adequate conditions of voluntariness and informed consent. As we have outlined in detail in Chapter 2, it is not obvious that such conditions are often adequately met for many recruits. This, however, is a separate issue for the reader to consider; all we aim to establish in this chapter is the conceptual possibility of initially supererogatory one-off acts transforming into ongoing morally exploitative relationships.

Given the existence of what we see as an ongoing and worsening morally exploitative relationship between present-day American civilians and soldiers, we argue that such a state of affairs gives some moral motivation for a draft or conscription model of military service. We will outline the specifics of this particular view in Chapter 5. For now, having addressed this issue of supererogation and outlining the scope and breadth of duties of citizenship, let us turn to consider in the next chapter some wider political and societal connections and downstream effects related to the present civil/military division of labor.

4

Connections

We have always been at war with Eastasia.

—*George Orwell, 1984*

Introduction

Now that we have investigated the moral exploitation of soldiers and the shared duties of citizenship, this chapter will focus on exploring a set of connections closely related to these two concepts. Some of these connections are obvious. Some of them are not. If the earlier chapters of this book dealt with the moral exploitation of soldiers directly, then this chapter will focus on some of the downstream and related second- and third-order effects of our presently lopsided division of moral labor with respect to war-fighting. By outlining this series of connections and related concepts, the overall shape, severity, and salience of the moral exploitation of soldiers will be brought further to light, and proper and relevant prescriptions and institutional reforms will hopefully become sharper and clearer. Broadly speaking these related areas of concern include (1) veteran's issues, (2) future military technologies and warfare, and (3) the global war on terror. Whereas the first set of related moral concerns affect present soldiers and veterans, the latter two areas affect future soldiers and veterans. Let us investigate each of these areas in turn.

Outsourcing Duty. Michael J. Robillard and Bradley J. Strawser, Oxford University Press. © Oxford University Press 2022. DOI: 10.1093/oso/9780190671457.003.0005

Veterans

Warfighters

To begin, let us look at one of the more obvious downstream consequences related to the moral exploitation of soldiers. Namely, the plight of the American veteran. Once again, our aim here is not to paint a picture of the American veteran as a helpless, broken victim. Rather, the hope is to take a sober and honest look at a constellation of phenomena within society connected to our nation's collective warfighting decisions and the slim portion of citizens within society who live out and bear the weight of those collective decisions. Being careful not to overstate the case, our claim is that the heaping moral (not just physical and psychological) burdens onto soldiers, especially over the last twenty years, can and likely does contribute, at least in part, to the creation and exacerbation of many of the psychological and social maladies plaguing the contemporary American veteran community. It would be surprising, in fact, if the two phenomena were not connected, perhaps directly. This claim finds greater credence especially when we consider the inverse relationship that has existed since World War II between decreasing relative soldier exposure to direct combat scenarios and increasing reports of various psychological ills among returning veterans.[1] Our claim is further reinforced by recent empirical findings of psychological trauma particularly in drone and reaper pilots who experience such psychological maladies in the complete absence of immediate environmental threat, the presumed cause of such phenomena. The fact that such psychological trends occur despite the diminishment of physical threats suggest that soldiers' minds and hearts are apprehending something beyond mere environmental danger.

[1] David Grossman, *On Killing* (New York, 1995).

One notable concept that has found increased attention in recent years within discussion and discourse surrounding veteran and soldier well-being is the concept of moral injury. Not to conflate moral injury with moral exploitation, these ideas nonetheless share several common aspects. To quote the Shay Moral Injury Center: "Moral injury is the damage done to one's conscience or moral compass when that person perpetrates, witnesses, or fails to prevent acts that transgress one's own moral beliefs, values, or ethical codes of conduct."[2] Offering an explicit definition of his own, psychiatrist Jonathan Shay writes that his "current most precise (and narrow) definition of moral injury has three parts. Moral injury is present when 1.) there has been a betrayal of what is morally correct 2.) by someone who holds legitimate authority 3.) in a high-stakes situation."[3] Lastly, echoing similar sentiments, philosopher Nancy Sherman writes:

> The term "moral injury" resonates with these troops. It's an old concept. The notion of a wound that is moral, or occasioned by "contempt" and "injustice," is the centerpiece of sermons by Bishop Joseph Butler in early 18th century England. From the philosopher's perspective, the concept is a way of talking about anguish caused by wrongdoing (real and perceived)—others toward you, you toward others, others toward others, you toward yourself. Agent, victim and witness are all players in the moral conscience. And transgression isn't the only issue at the heart of moral injury. So is falling short of the lofty ideals of military honor. That the military code—never abandon a buddy, bring all

---

[2] "What Is Moral Injury?" The Shay Moral Injury Center online content, accessed November 1, 2021, https://www.voa.org/moral-injury-war-inside?gclid=CjwKCAjw4MP5BRBtEiwAS fwAL7JH0H54A9XSjHSb0CSb5Luipqwi7aMVrKRKknl_qsx6kzOsismpuhoCRb4QAvD_ BwE.

[3] J. Shay and J. Munroe, "Group and Milieu Therapy for Veterans with Complex Posttraumatic Stress Disorder," in *Posttraumatic Stress Disorder: A Comprehensive Text*, ed. Philip A. Saigh and J. Douglas Bremner (Boston, 1998) 391–413.

your troops home, don't put innocents at risk—is impossible to meet doesn't always register deep down. The result may be shame, and all too often suicidal shame.

She continues:

Moral injury is distinct from post-traumatic stress disorder, which is generally thought of narrowly as a fear-conditioned syndrome marked by hyper-vigilance and flashbacks. The prevailing treatment for PTSD is therapy to "decondition" the fear response. But guilt, shame, raging resentment and betrayal are different from fear. To overcome them requires relationships that rebuild a soldier's sense of trust in himself and others, no small order given the effects of war.[4]

Reported cases of moral injury have often revolved around veteran testimony surrounding cases of personal responsibility such as cases of killing/injuring the enemy, disproportionate violence, harming civilians and civilian life, and failing to prevent harm to others, as well as responsibility in the form of testimony of disproportionate violence, , betrayal by trusted others, and betrayal by trusted systems and institutions. Moral injury often brings on a sense of demoralization and self-condemnation, two factors often associated with depression. Shame is also thought to be a link between the transgressive act of moral injury and depression and manifests even those not in direct combat experience.

As we shall see, the dual concepts of moral exploitation and moral injury both mutually inform one another. For instance, the moral exploitation of soldiers provides one plausible explanatory backstory as to how moral injury occurs and eventuates. That is, our

---

[4] Nancy Sherman, "The Deepest War Wound May Be the Anguish of Moral Injury," *LA Times*, April 24, 2015, https://www.law.upenn.edu/live/files/4750-nancy-sherman-moral-injury-la-timespdf.

account paints a picture of how the very same set of moral values and idealisms initially motivating a person to join at the time of recruitment can later turn in on themselves, sometimes violently and viciously so, when confronted with the vagaries of actual combat, the result then being a kind of internal wounding of sorts. Conversely, the heightened likelihood of exposure to moral-injury-laden combat scenarios provides one reason for nations to curtail or reform potentially exploitative relations and institutions within society that unfairly or disproportionately expose only a small portion of its overall population to such harrowing and demanding moral situations.

Lastly, the often silent and invisible carrying of dirty hands; hands disproportionately sullied on behalf of a largely apathetic and otherwise "morally clean" public might serve as a partial explanation of not just moral injury but also other related social and psychological ills within the greater veteran community. Indeed, related statistical data having to do with veteran PTSD, homelessness, drug and alcohol abuse, criminality, divorce, homicide, suicide, and general veteran testimony of societal alienation all serve as additional indicators of something drastically amiss in our country's collective relationship to its servicemen and women.[5] As noted previously, these statistics are especially vexing and even more perplexing considering the overall decrease in soldier exposure to battlefield contexts involving immediate physical threat, kinetic harm, or trigger-pulling.

Thumos, Recognition Self-Respect, and Self-Regarding Duties

Closely tied to the phenomena of moral exploitation and moral injury in soldiers is the concept of *thumos* (or *thymos*). *Thumos*, in

---

[5] See "Suicide and Homeless Veterans," report from VA National Center on Homelessness Among Veterans, US Department of Veteran Affairs, February 27, 2018, https://www.va.gov/HOMELESS/nchav/research/HERS6_Suicide.asp. See also, "Homeless Evidence and Research Synthesis (HERS) Roundtable Proceedings," US Department of Veteran Affairs, February 27, 2018, https://www.va.gov/HOMELESS/nchav/docs/HERS_Proceedings_SuicideAndHomelessVeteransSymposium_Feb2018_508.pdf.

the classic Greek, roughly translates to the notion of "inner spir-itedness, passion" or "fire in the belly," as well as a demand from others that one's basic human dignity be properly recognized and respected. One could call it a kind of insistence by one of one's own wroth. Plato famously conceived of *thumos* (passion), along with *nous* (reason), and *eros* (bodily appetite), to comprise the so-called tripartite division of the soul, corresponding metaphorically with the bodily organs of head, heart, and stomach respectively. Political theorist, Francis Fukuyama, in his classic *The End of History and the Last Man,* argued that there were two expressions of *thymos* in modern political life: *isothymia* and *megalothymia. Isothymia* refers to the need to be recognized as merely equal to others in terms of basic human dignity and respect, while *megalothymia* refers to the need to be recognized as superior to others.[6]

Within this same general conceptual space, we find similarity within Aristotelian virtue ethics. In his famous *Nichomachean Ethics,* Aristotle formulates *virtue* as being a "golden mean" met-aphysically situated between the *vices* of deficiency and excess. For Aristotle, the virtue of courage, for instance, is located be-tween the excess of recklessness and the deficiency of cowardice. Similarly, the virtue of friendliness is located between the excess of obsequiousness and the deficiency of cantankerousness.[7] And for our purposes here, particularly in relation to *thumos*, the virtue of magnanimity (i.e., self-worth, personal pride, and self-respect) is located between the excess of delusions of grandeur and the defi-ciency of self-abnegation or martyrdom.

Commercial Surrogate Mothers

Closely overlapping concepts can also be found in contemporary applied ethics, particularly contemporary feminist ethics with

---

[6] Francis Fukuyama, *The End of History and the Last Man Free Press* (New York, 1992).

[7] Aristotle, *Nichomachean Ethics.*

respect to the exploitation of commercial surrogate mothers. In her essay, "Buns in the Oven: Objectification, Surrogacy, and Women's Autonomy," philosopher Suze Berkhout makes the distinction between *recognition* self-respect and *estimative* self-respect. She writes:

> Generally, there are two forms of respect considered in self-respect discourse. I contend that both kinds of self-respect play a significant role in how objectification in commercial surrogacy diminishes autonomy, and why it may be surreptitious in some instances. Recognition self-respect entails appropriate consideration of one's personhood; in being a form of respect that is owed to all persons qua persons, recognition self-respect requires that the holder take seriously the facts of his/her humanity. As it relates to one's status worth as a person, recognition self-respect will at least depend on one's ability to see oneself and act in a way that is reflective of one's equality, agency, and individuality (with respect to a Western conception of persons, at any rate). Appraisal, or estimative self-respect, refers to the esteem that accompanies one's accomplishments, a merit-based form of respect.[8]

Berkhout argues that the traditional morality of many surrogate mothers often heightens a surrogate's estimative self-respect while severely diminishing or debilitating her basic sense of recognition self-respect. Interviews with commercial surrogate mothers, Berkhout notes, often report subjective testimony of elation and extreme joy over lending their physical bodies and gestational labor to help perform/accomplish the birth of the surrogate baby. At the same time, however, Berkhout notes that these same interviewees seemed to show very little signs of basic recognition self-respect

---

[8] Suze G. Berkhout, "Buns in the Oven: Objectification, Surrogacy, and Women's Autonomy," *Social Theory and Practice*, 34, no. 1 (2008), 95–117. For soldiers, estimative self-respect is often heightened by way of awards and medals, sometimes to the detriment or de-prioritization of one's recognition respect.

(i.e., little or no concern over their bodily autonomy being used purely instrumentally, little to no concern for their womb being commodified, and little to no entertaining the idea that they might be getting exploited or taken advantage of that they could or even should negotiate for a better deal in such market transactions).

In this sense, there are many strong parallels between the seeming lack of *thumos*, magnanimity, and recognition respect displayed in both contemporary veterans and commercial surrogate mothers. This lack of recognition respect is arguably made possible, at least in part, by virtue of the traditional values of charity, self-sacrifice, and altruism taken to excess in both demographics. This arguably then sets up situations for the overburdening, exploiting, or taking advantage of such vulnerable groups. For young recruits in particular, sublimation of the basic instinct toward self-regard and recognition respect begins, at first, by way of their initial contractual entrance into the military institution. This sublimation is then further reinforced by instrumentalization of bodily autonomy during basic training and the subsequent compounding of moral burdens—sometimes for an entire military career. Continued sublimation of basic instincts for self-regard, recognition self-respect, and proper *thumos* often persist long after a veteran's official exit from the military institution.

The conflicting sense of honoring a duty to one's self to assert one's own basic recognition respect while at the same time honoring a competing previously stated duty to honor the virtues of "selflessness," "sacrifice," and "putting the team and the mission first" often leaves many soldiers and veterans deeply internally conflicted about discerning *isothymia* from *megalothymia*, magnanimity from selfishness, and selflessness from self-abnegation. This feeling of inner conflict is further exacerbated by the soldier's or veteran's return to domesticated civilian society at times at odds with proper recognition respect toward them. At least as things presently stand in American civilian society, soldiers or veterans are often told, either implicitly or explicitly by some subset of their fellow countrymen whom their service has protected, that they are little more than "oppressors" and thereby deserve no public expression of recognition respect whatsoever. (This view is most often tied to justifiable objections to bellicose American foreign policy.) This institutionalized deficiency in recognition self-respect, sadly, often finds parallel expression in many military spouses, especially military wives.

Indeed, the fact that military spouses in particular are, statistically speaking, the most sought-after demographic for commercial surrogacy in the United States lends further credence to the these claims. The outsized role military spouses play in this set is truly noteworthy. According to one UK *Telegraph* report, "20 percent of the surrogate babies born in America each year are carried by military wives, a cohort that represents *less than one percent* of the female population of childbearing age."[9] Given that, on the whole, married couples in general tend to be strongly similar in terms of age, socioeconomic class, geographic region, education level, and values, military wives will likely share many of the same traditional values of altruism, selflessness, and self-sacrifice bordering on martyrdom as those of their military counterparts.

Similar to their military partners, a surrogate's more "traditional" values outlook might function to make her considerably more vulnerable to exploitation than one might think. Indeed, just as military recruiters select recruits who show strong signs of altruism, so too do many surrogacy agencies. This high premium placed on the virtues of selflessness and altruism permeates the language and testimonies of both soldiers and surrogates alike.

For example, Berkhout notes that one surrogate, commenting on her motivations, stated, "I wanted to do the ultimate thing for somebody, to give them the ultimate. Nobody can beat that,

---

[9] Sally Howard, "US Army Wives: The Most Sought-After Surrogates in the World," *The Telegraph*, May 7, 2015, https://www.telegraph.co.uk/women/mother-tongue/11583 541/US-army-wives-the-most-sought-after-surrogates-in-the-world.html.

nobody can do anything nicer for them."[10] Similarly, in other surrogacy communities we also find similar language of "mothers
helping mothers." Such an emphasis on the virtue of altruism,
Berkhout argues, ultimately results in a dichotomy between the
"pure" surrogate and the "wicked" surrogate. In public discourse,
surrogates are dichotomized as "pure" or "wicked"; good and bad
rely on the idea that altruism and remuneration are mutually exclusive. Stigmatization is thus associated with the presumed moral
character of the surrogate—a negative evaluation of the commercial elements of surrogacy are prominent. These dichotomous
tropes lend themselves to the strong use of gift language and the
emphasis on altruism by those in the industry, especially by the surrogate mothers.[11]

Wertheimer echoes a similar sentiment when he considers how
the mere offering of more monetary compensation to surrogates
often problematizes the situation by stigmatizing the surrogate
rather than making matters better. He writes, "I suspect that higher
pay is not offered as a solution to the problem of exploitation in part
because the very receipt of monetary compensation may actually
cause some of the psychological harm experienced by some surrogate mothers, who may feel they are doing something 'sleazy.' "[12]
Such considerations about non-altruistically motivated surrogates
bring us back to our earlier points regarding non-altruistically
motivated soldiers and connotations typically associated with the
word "mercenary."

Just as suggesting that soldiers are primarily motivated by
self-interested gains like monetary compensation, job skills, or

---

[10] Suze G. Berkhout, "Reproductive Autonomy on the Cutting Edge," *American Journal of Bioethics* 12, no. 7 (2012): 59. See also, Suze G. Berkhout, "Buns in the Oven: Objectification, Surrogacy, and Women's Autonomy," *Social Theory and Practice* 34, no. 1 (2008): 95–117.

[11] Berkhout, "Reproductive Autonomy on the Cutting Edge."

[12] Alan Wertheimer, "Exploitation and Commercial Surrogacy," *Denver Law Review* 74, no. 4 (January 1997): 1218. See also, Alan Wertheimer, "Two Questions about Surrogacy and Exploitation," *Philosophy and Public Affairs* 21, no. 3 (1992): 211–39.

educational benefit connotes a kind of moral deficiency, one that often severely constrains a soldier's negotiating power with the military, a similar tactic seems to be employed by many surrogacy agencies when recruiting surrogates and when negotiating with surrogates throughout the duration of the surrogacy contract. Not wanting to appear selfish or "sleazy," and often ascribing to more traditional deferential roles, surrogates often find themselves in situations where demanding greater compensation or sticking up for themselves runs contrary to their stated traditional values of service. And likewise, sadly, often with their military husbands.

Future Military Technologies and Warfare

A second area of ethical concern connected to the moral exploitation of soldiers is the space of emerging military technologies and future warfare. While this book has focused on the aspect and character of present-day moral burdens shouldered by many soldiers, the space of emerging technologies and future warfare will certainly function as a new frontier rife with new moral burdens, dilemmas, and complexities for soldiers to navigate. As discussed earlier, with a societal trend towards an ever-widening civil-military divide, like two diverging paths on a forked road, the moral burdens and dirty hands scenarios endemic to future warfighting technologies, means, and methods will predictably be shouldered by an even thinner slice of the American populous than at present. Let us look at some of these emerging warfighting technologies, and some of the possible moral quandaries they raise.

Soldier Enhancement

One ethically laden area related to future military technologies is the fast-emerging space of "soldier enhancement." As with today's military technology, this area of moral concern is similarly fraught with new and unique moral demands facing present and future soldiers, particularly with respect to demands upon a soldier's character and identity. By soldier enhancement we broadly mean technological enhancement or augmentation of otherwise natural human abilities and capacities by means of artificial technological intervention. To borrow a working definition from ethicist Pat Lin:

> We will operate under the working definition that an enhancement is a medical or biological intervention to the body designed "to improve performance, appearance, or capability besides what is necessary to achieve, sustain or restore health."[13]

This would then include such areas as genetic enhancement, man-machine pairing, bio-enhancement, and cognitive and neurological enhancement. These new and emerging technologies in the space of soldier enhancement engender a number of moral worries and concerns worth thinking about. For starters, one salient moral issue surrounding soldier enhancement is the issue of informed consent. Unlike standard conceptions of warfare and soldiering, the newly emerging and experimental world of soldier bio-enhancement might entail a whole new set of cognitive, epistemic, and moral demands that young recruits might not be able to conceive of or envision at the time of recruitment. Furthermore, once a soldier is enhanced with new and potentially unforeseen physical or cognitive abilities, the latent moral demands, risks, and responsibilities might reveal themselves over time in ways detrimental to and unpredictable for the enhanced soldier.

A second issue surrounding soldier enhancement are the dual concepts of character and identity. If one is subject to any number

[13] Patrick Lin, Maxwell Mehlman, and Keith Abney, "Enhanced Warfigthers: Risk, Ethics, and Policy," Report prepared for The Greenwall Foundation, January 1, 2013, http://ethics.calpoly.edu/Greenwall_report.pdf.

of moral vagaries and dirty hands scenarios in combat, is it morally preferable for the soldier to silently sit with and reflect upon his actions or inactions, or is it preferable for him or her to take a cognitive drug such as the beta blocker propanol that has the potential psychological effect of decoupling strong emotions from the memory of a particular traumatic event? Is it best for a soldier's character and conscience that he or she be able to feel certain emotions accompanying a battlefield memory, or is it better for one's emotion and character to be chemically dampened? Lastly, what does such enhancement spell for identity and reintegration into civilian society? If one is transformed into a living bionic hero on the battlefield with superhuman robotic capacities, what does it do to that soldier's identity and sense of self when he must turn in his enhanced capacities and return to civilian live un-enhanced? Furthermore, if "ought implies can," one might wonder in such cases if "can implies ought." In other words, if a soldier is biologically enhanced such that he or she is one of the only persons in the country who can perform certain essential tasks and actions for the sake of the nation, is it ethically permissible for him or her to not re-enlist or to retire early into normal civilian life? Answering these questions sufficiently, of course, is still very much an open question for many ethicists, policymakers, and military leaders. That being said, the main point is that the distribution of moral burdens, challenges, and dilemmas endemic to these new and potentially risky technologies, if things don't institutionally change, will predictably be inherited by only a thin sliver of the overall populace once again.

Soft War

A second morally and epistemically ambiguous area that present and future soldiers will have to soon inherit is that of so-called soft war. Soft war, broadly speaking, involves a number of fundamentally non-kinetic means and methods of warfare below the level of armed conflict. Soft war can therefore involve things such as PSYOP (psychological operations), informational warfare and propaganda, weaponized media and journalism, election hacking, troll farms, deep fakes, disinformation campaigns, cyberattacks and hacking, lawfare, economic warfare, and the use of NGOs (non-governmental organizations) as a means and cover for state subversion. Unlike conventional forms of warfare involving physically crossing territorial boundaries as well as the kinetic harming of combatants and/or equipment and infrastructure, the space of soft war involves neither of these elements. Accordingly, since soft-war strategies and tactics involve neither the overt crossing of territorial boundaries, and hence *ad bellum* ethical considerations, nor direct kinetic attacks, hence *in bello* ethical considerations, it is unclear how the standard just war frameworks of *jus ad bellum* and *jus in bello* apply to the domain of soft war, if at all.

The fast and growing area of soft war therefore opens up new and important ethical problems, dilemmas, and questions that present and future soldiers will have to soon deal with, such as the following:

How do we conceive of territorial aggression for a cyberattack that technically crosses no physical territorial boundaries?

How do we assign liability to third-party groups and nations who own the servers that terrorist groups use to launch a hacking attack?

How do we conceive of "collateral damage" and noncombatant discrimination when it comes to the employment of such soft-war methods?

How should we conceive of harmful second-order effects that occur downstream from initial non-kinetic attacks?

What kind, amount, or aggregation of non-kinetic soft-war attacks justifies a kinetic response?

Indeed, ethics debates surrounding these questions are still very much in their infancy. Regardless, much like the issue of soldier bio-enhancement, so too will the area of soft war bring with it a whole new set of nuanced, complicated, and likely compounding ethical entanglements that soldiers and soldiers alone will have to deal with.

Autonomous Weapons Systems (AWS)

A final, highly controversial area in the space of emerging military technologies and warfare is that of autonomous weapons systems (AWS). Unlike "semi-autonomous" weapons such as some present drone technology, fully autonomous weapons are, at least in principle, understood to operate wholly independent of human decision-making.

In a 2012 directive, the US Department of Defense (DoD) defined an autonomous weapon system as the following:

A weapon system that, once activated, can select and engage targets without further intervention by a human operator. This includes human-supervised autonomous weapon systems that are designed to allow human operators to override operation of the weapon system, but can select and engage targets without further human input after activation.[14]

Homing in further on a working and substantive definition of AWS, ethicist Suzanne Burri in "What Is the Moral Problem with Killer Robots?" states:

Autonomous weapons have, in a sense, existed with us for some time now. Anti-personnel mines, for instance, arguably "select"

[14] DoD Directive Number 3000.09, US Department of Defense November 21, 2012, https://www.esd.whs.mil/portals/54/documents/dd/issuances/dodd/300009p.pdf.

their own targets once a human has primed them. The Israeli Harpy, a loitering anti-radar missile, deploys without a specifically designated target, flies a search pattern, identifies an enemy radar and then divebombs and destroys it. However, policymakers and ethicists are not primarily concerned about these kinds of autonomous weapons. They are instead concerned about weapons systems of much greater technical sophistication.[15]

For many people—ethicists, soldiers, and laypersons alike—there seems to be a strong moral repulsion about the idea of using such weapons in war. Some of this repulsion is due to a series of contingent concerns about such things as incentivization for overuse by political leaders, ease of accessibility for terrorists and nonstate actors, proliferation, lack of accountability, the danger of malfunction, or even existential risk. Conversely, some of this repulsion regarding AWS is due to in-principle moral reasons having to do with inherent "responsibility gaps," morality's irreducibility to formal algorithmic codification, and deontological objections based on respect for the dignity of human combatants.

And while debates over these contingent and in-principle worries surrounding AWS continue to play out among academics, lawmakers, and tech experts at the heights of idealization, rest assured, present and future soldiers will likely be the exclusive inheritors and stewards of such idealizations tasked to supervise, implement, and own the messy real-world battlefield results (and accidents). In this sense, we can think of the emergence of AWS as being the next logical progression of the institutional "outsourcing" of the messy moral consequences of America's wars pushed even further out of sight and out of mind behind a sanitized veil of machine complexity, silicon, and algorithms.

[15] Suzanne Burri, "What Is the Moral Problem with Killer Robots?," in *Who Should Die: Liability and Killing in War?*, ed. Ryan Jenkins, Michael Robillard, and Bradley Strawser (Oxford, 2017).

The Global War on Terror

As a final relevant connection to the moral exploitation of soldiers, let us look at the so-called global war on terror that America has been waging for the last twenty years without pause and with no clear end in sight. Sometimes referred to as the "Forever War," unlike any of America's previous wars since its founding, the veterans of this generation's particular wars have not yet seen an actual or official or even ambiguous unofficial end to the wars they started. A 2020 Military.com article underlines this point starkly. The piece "Years After They Fought in Afghanistan, US Troops Watch Their Children Deploy to the Same War" reports the harrowing testimonies of a military father and son who both deployed to Afghanistan at different phases of the war's development. That article states:

> The elder Mavalwalla, 55, a former captain, said the country has made great strides since he first served there in 2002 with the 19th Special Forces Group.

> "Afghanistan didn't have a functioning toilet when I showed up," he said. When he returned in 2012 as an advisor to police in the western city of Herat, the improvements were "unbelievable," he said.

> But his son, who was barely a teenager when his father first went to Afghanistan, said he was disillusioned when he deployed to Kandahar province in 2012 with the 250th Military Intelligence Battalion.

> "I wanted to go out and help people, serve my country . . . (but) I just sort of contributed to this deepening mire," he said.[16]

---

[16] J. P. Lawrence and Philli Walter Wellman, "Years After They Fought in Afghanistan, US Troops Watch as Their Children Deploy to Same War," *Military Times,* October 7, 2020, https://www.military.com/daily-news/2020/10/07/years-after-they-fought-afgh anistan-us-troops-watch-their-children-deploy-same-war.html.

Indeed, since 9/11, the mission creep merry-go-round of moral and political justifications for a continued US military presence and ongoing warfighting in the Middle East has switched so often and for so long over the past two decades, it is honestly hard for one to remember and keep track of them—and we are academic experts who follow and analyze such justifications professionally. From initial justification for violence based on reprisal against al-Qaeda and the Taliban (and thereby appeals to future deterrence justification); to reports of Saddam Hussein's possession of WMDs (and hence an appeal to imminent threat justification); to the moral necessity for "regime change" in Iraq; to Colin Powell's "we broke it, we bought it" justification for continued military presence in the area despite the war's questionable moral beginnings; to a perpetual preventative posture during the Obama administration of indefinitely "keeping the terrorists on the backfoot"; to appeals to UN "nation-building" in the Middle East; to the necessity to spread liberal democracy; to continuing onward for the sake of retroactively recouping sunk costs on the back end once the war is finally won in some far off, distant, and unspecified future—for all of these reasons—America's Forever War has continued ad nauseum while the goalposts of mission success and finality forever shift along with it.

To make matters worse, this mission creep in justification has continued unabated while critical public engagement pertaining to the war and its consequences, both domestically and abroad, has crept further and further into the background of the social imagination. This normalization—of increased public apathy and civilian blindness to the war and its consequences—is made evermore vexing by the near constant loop of surface-level and faux displays of authentic public regard often in the form of discount veteran deals, monetary incentives "for the troops," and halftime sports celebrations of the sort previously alluded to in Fountain's *Billy Lynn's Long Halftime Walk* and Bacevich's *Breach of Trust*. Such normalization carries with it several other deep and morally pernicious worries for Americans and America's future beyond the effects on just veterans.

Specifically, another moral worry highlighted by our present public apathy toward America's veterans and its ongoing wars is the question of transmission of social knowledge and narrative between and across generations. Indeed, it seems evident that throughout history certain crises and traumas to political and social groups can take on their own unique kind of causal power and can be transmitted and passed on to future individuals and groups. This transmission of narrative can occur until the trauma overtakes the saliency of original memories and reasons underpinning group behaviors, norms, and ways of social life.[17] The trauma can, in effect, rise to the level of a new default meta-narrative and organizing social myth, inherited as completely normal by new generations of citizens who know no different. In past generations, "fear of the atomic bomb," or "the red scare" might have filled this role of meta-narrative to organize and marshal civil and military resources in American society. This organizing social narrative was then arguably replaced, at least in part, by the war on drugs, and later, by the open-ended war on terror.

This isn't to downplay the actuality or severity of threats posed by the likes of al-Qaeda and its affiliates or the very real dangers that other terrorist groups pose across the world. Rather, the main point here is to point out how certain traumatic events (such as the attacks on 9/11) can cause society to seize up and have the memories of those traumas echo through social institutions for years to come, thereby generating a sort of institutional momentum and causal power of its own long after the initial incident. One needn't posit some shadowy cabal to explain such phenomena. Rather this

---

[17] Case in point: In October 2020, the *New York Times* announced the official discontinuation of its "At War" column that had started commenting on the global war on terror in 2009. See Lauren Katzenberg, "Turning the Lights Down on the at War Channel," *New York Times Magazine,* October 16, 2020, https://www.nytimes.com/2020/10/16/magazine/at-war-channel.html.

effect seems to be the typical logic of how large-scale institutions and bureaucracies respond to such traumas and crises over time. In his book review of Matt Farwel and Michael Ames's "American Cypher," Major Nicholas Utzig's describes this emergent phenomenon as follows:

> The United States' longest war—nearly absent, Farwell and Ames note, from the political conversation during the 2016 presidential election (a judgment the pair might also apply to the 2018 election cycle)—shows no sign of ending any time soon. The war perpetuates itself out of bureaucratic inertia.[18]

It is this last line of Utzig's passage that we should take most seriously: The war itself and its related political, military, financial, and social institutions could function as an independent and sui generis source of its own perpetuation, separate and distinct from the direct volition, knowledge, and causal agency of any set of individual actors or groups. That being said, there clearly *are* stakeholders and interest groups, of course, that do indeed benefit from such momentum continuing rather than ceasing.

Made popular by President Dwight D. Eisenhower's now famous farewell speech, the notorious "military-industrial complex" (MIC) refers to the relationship between the vast private sector and government machinery that is brought to bear on American foreign policy and military spending. To quote Eisenhower:

> In the councils of government, we must guard against the acquisition of unwarranted influence, whether sought or unsought, by the military–industrial complex. The potential for the disastrous

---

[18] Nicholas Utzig, "Five Years Gone: What Bowe Bergdahl's Odyssey Tells Us About the United States's Endless War in Afghanistan," *Los Angeles Review of Book,* May 30, 2019, https://lareviewofbooks.org/article/five-years-gone-what-bowe-bergdahls-odyssey-tells-us-about-the-united-statess-endless-war-in-afghanistan/. We note that the absence was also notable in the 2020 election.

rise of misplaced power exists, and will persist. We must never let the weight of this combination endanger our liberties or democratic processes. We should take nothing for granted. Only an alert and knowledgeable citizenry can compel the proper meshing of the huge industrial and military machinery of defense with our peaceful methods and goals so that security and liberty may prosper together.[19]

The impact and enduring inertial force of the MIC can be seen through what is referred to as the "iron triangle," or the set of institutional relationships that exist between the House and Senate Committees on Armed Services, the DoD, and the private defense industry, which includes endless defense contractors and well-paid lobbying groups. This ongoing relationship can involve not only undue influence on foreign policy decision-making but also the circulation of funding, political support, favors, legislation, and even transfers of personnel (i.e., the so-called revolving door) to serve the interests of the stakeholders involved.

The prescience of Eisenhower's warning to the American public is as remarkable as it is tragic. Arguably on its third iteration now, the MIC continues to exert strong and significant influence on military spending and strategic thinking as America proceeds into its twentieth consecutive year of the global war on terror. Eisenhower's warning has not gone wholly unheard. Contemporary political scholar, Andrew Bacevich, in his 2011 *Atlantic* article, "The Tyranny of Defense Inc.," reiterates many of Ike's sentiments when commenting on present-day military spending. To quote Bacevich: "By diverting social capital from productive to destructive purposes, war and the preparation for war deplete, rather than enhance, a nation's strength."[20]

[19] Eisenhower.
[20] Bacevich, "The Tyranny of Defense Inc.," *Atlantic*, February 15, 2011.

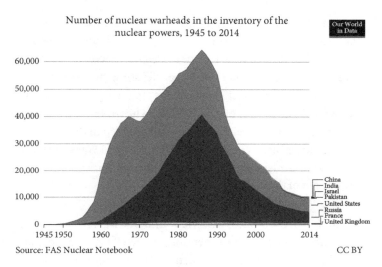

Figure 4.1 Number of nuclear warheads in the inventory of the nuclear powers, 1945 to 2014.

One significant data set that Bacevich points to that demonstrates this trend is the growth of the US nuclear stockpile from 1,000 warheads in 1952, to 24,000 in 1961, to a peak of 61,000 nuclear warheads in 1986 (see Figure 4.1).

According to Bacevich, support for the MIC hinges on two major theoretical concepts:

1. Military metaphysics
2. Military Keynesianism

Military metaphysics (coined by C. Wright Mills) is the view that war is an international reality and that peace is merely a transition period between wars. Bacevich criticizes the MIC for deliberately generating public fear of war, particularly with Afghanistan and China in recent years, to justify unnecessary military spending.[21] He wrote:

---

[21] Bacevich, "The Tyranny of Defense Inc."

The threat inflation that led to the bomber and missile "gaps" of the 1950s remains a cherished Washington tradition. In memos written after September 11, then–Defense Secretary Donald Rumsfeld urged his staff to "keep elevating the threat" and demanded "bumper sticker statements" to gin up public enthusiasm for the global war on terror. The key, he wrote, was to "make the American people realize they are surrounded in the world by violent extremists." What worked during the Cold War still works today: to get Americans on board with your military policy, scare the hell out of them.[22]

Going further, on Bacevich's view, military Keynesianism is the idea that increasing military spending will itself cause an economic boom. This idea largely gained traction after the post–World War II economic boom in America, and for good reason.

Yet Bacevich contends, rightly, that this idea crumbles in the modern era. Unlike in the 1950s, the United States now imports far more than we export, and our continuous wars mean that our military products go abroad and never return home. Indeed, Bacevich notes that just to train, equip, and maintain one American soldier in Afghanistan costs $1,000,000. Meanwhile, a 2010 US census report showed the number of Americans falling below the poverty line is one in every seven, while the estimated cost of the wars in the Middle East is usually pegged at somewhere around $6.5 trillion over the past twenty years.[23] Noting these shocking trends in US military spending, Bacevich ends by reiterating the same general sentiment as Eisenhower some sixty years prior: American citizens need to better regulate such funding because the executive powers are being pigeon-holed by the overwhelming influence of the MIC (see Figure 4.2 for US defense spending).[24]

---

[22] Bacevich, "The Tyranny of Defense Inc."

[23] Amanda Macias, "America Has Spent $6.4 Trillion on Wars in the Middle East and Asia since 2001, a New Study Says," *CNBC*, November 20, 2019, https://www.cnbc.com/2019/11/20/us-spent-6point4-trillion-on-middle-east-wars-since-2001-study.html.

[24] This influence of the MIC is perhaps most strikingly exemplified by (then) Vice President Dick Cheyney's connection to the contracting company Haliburton during

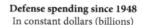

Defense spending since 1948
In constant dollars (billions)

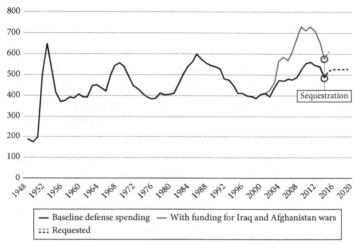

Source: Defense spending data from U.S. Department of Defense.

Figure 4.2   Defense spending since 1948.

Thus, the net consequence of this combination of rudderless momentum, special interest groups, and the echoes of institutional trauma has, for the most part, resulted in a "one foot in the boat, one foot on the shore" strategic posture for the United States with respect to the Middle East for (at least) the past two decades and over three distinct administrations. The other peculiar result of this amalgamation of factors has been political elements of both the establishment right and the establishment left, in large part, delivering roughly the same foreign policy prescriptions regardless of political administration. The Bush and Obama administrations

the initial invasion of the Iraq War. At the beginning of the war, Halliburton was able to score high-paying open-ended contracts. Its Pentagon contracts were $483 million in 2002 and over $6 billion in 2006 (according to annual editions of the DoD document, "100 Companies Receiving the Largest Dollar Volume of Prime Contract Awards." Billions of dollars that Halliburton received is still considered unaccounted for as the Pentagon reduced the number of contracting officers during this time.

delivered roughly the same foreign policy prescriptions in the Middle East with a few adjustments save perhaps for the increased use of drones and special forces with respect to the latter. More broadly, proponents of US neo-conservatism or UN-style cosmopolitanism continue to deliver the same general US foreign policy prescriptions. That is, never-ending US presence in the Middle East. This surprisingly unified front on our bellicose state of affairs is perhaps most poignantly displayed by the likes of even Noam Chomsky, perennial critic of US militarism, agitating for continued US involvement in Syria.[25]

Even if one were to somehow bracket this long history aside, a solid case can be independently made that the war on terror —from its shifting moral justifications to its overarching grand strategy— has become handmaiden to big business, lobbying groups, foreign influence, as well as simply blind institutional momentum with no one's hand firmly on the rudder. Accordingly, be it neo-conservative war hawks, cosmopolitan UN lawmakers, left-leaning academics, alphabet soup DoD agencies, Raytheon, Haliburton, Kuwait, Israel, or the Saudi royal family, the very same prescription repeats itself time and time again: *"Send in the troops."* It doesn't seem like a stretch to speculate that the absence of "skin in the game" for the average American civilian—or average American politician for that matter—likely significantly contributes to this ongoing and never-ending strategic quagmire.[26] It is hard to imagine this state of affairs continuing unabated as it has, were the burdens of war shared by a broader basis of Americans.

---

[25] Wladimir van Wilgenburg, "Noam Chomsky Says US Should Stay in Syria to Protect the Kurds," *Kurdistan 24 News,* October 3, 2018, https://www.kurdistan24.net/en/news/13cf816e-8e40-41c8-bb76-d453a3261d8b.

[26] From Alexander the Great to the British in 1800s to Soviet Russia in the 1980s, Afghanistan has perennially been referred to by historians and military thinkers alike as the "Graveyard of Empires"

Conclusion

While the moral connections and concerns addressed in this chapter are not immediately caused by the moral exploitation of soldiers, they nonetheless constitute a network of related themes pointing to the downstream negative effects of our present civil-military scheme. These truths bear themselves out both officially in the organs of government and unofficially in terms of mainstream society and culture. Coupled with the moral exploitation of soldiers, this set of related moral and societal concerns warrants greater attention in terms of institutional reform. There is, of course, much more to be said on this score. However, let us now move on to our final chapter to consider several normative prescriptions and conceptions of institutional reform in these areas. That is, let us consider, What can actually be done?

5

Prescriptions

Society can give its young men almost any job and they'll
figure how to do it. They'll suffer for it and die for it and
watch their friends die for it, but in the end, it will get done.
That only means that society should be careful about what
it asks for. . . . Soldiers themselves are reluctant to evaluate
the costs of war, but someone must. That evaluation, on-
going and unadulterated by politics, may be the one thing a
country absolutely owes the soldiers who defend its borders.
—Sebastian Junger, *War*

Introduction

America's civil-military relationship is at an impasse. The moral exploitation of America's soldiers coupled with nearly two decades of
ongoing expeditionary and adventurist Middle Eastern conflicts—
and the social, political, and moral consequences of their wake—
has brought our nation to a point of institutional tension in serious
need of reconciliation. This civil-military morass can arguably be
resolved in one of three major ways. This chapter will outline and
explore some of the major ethical and prudential implications,
both positive and negative, of each of these three major policy
prescriptions.

Broadly speaking, these policy options can be described as
follows:

Outsourcing Duty. Michael J. Robillard and Bradley J. Strawser, Oxford University Press. © Oxford
University Press 2022. DOI: 10.1093/oso/9780190671457.003.0006

1. Maintain the all-volunteer force, with or without reforms specifically in the areas of recruitment and compensation (what we will call here the *all-volunteer* option).

2. Shift back to a mandatory conscription or draft-based model of national service, to include military service (what we will call here the *skin in the game* option).

3. Create a new institutional policy option exclusively linking certain political and foreign policy decision-making to national military service. What we will call the *Butler* option, referring to Major General Smedley Butler and the set of institutional prescriptions outlined in his famous 1935 work *War Is a Racket*.

Let us now explore each of these policy prescriptions in turn.[1]

The All-Volunteer Option

The all-volunteer option has two versions: The version with reforms and the version without reforms. Since the all-volunteer option without reforms would be both uninteresting and contrary to the entire spirit of this book's thesis, let us move on then to consider what the specifics of the all-volunteer option with reforms might possibly look like. Given the moral exploitation of soldiers that we have here argued for, *if* America is to keep its current institutional scheme of an all-volunteer fighting force, we argue that institutional reform is strongly needed. We argue

---

[1] Arguably there is a fourth policy option with respect to present civil-military relations, what we might call the *Outsource to 11* option. This position argues that we should further outsource warfighting responsibilities on behalf of the demos to private military contractors. Given what we have outlined in Chapter 3 with respect to duties citizens have to one another and that soldiers have to the demos via state institutions (to include legitimate authority considerations), we believe that this option is morally untenable on our view. We will therefore not discuss it any further, though, of course the many ethical ins and outs of relying upon mercenaries is a complicated issue deserving its own thorough treatment. See Andrew Alexandra, Dean-Peter Baker, Marina Caparini, eds., *Private Military and Security Companies: Ethics, Policies, and Civil-Military Relations* (Milton Park, 2008).

that such reform should naturally parse into the areas of ex ante and ex post and more specifically into reforms concerning recruitment and compensation.

Recruitment Reform

With respect to recruitment reform, we argue that institutional reform of the all-volunteer force arguably should take place in the three major areas of recruitment: age, demographic targeting, and recruitment content. With respect to age, as we have argued here, we believe that the phenomenon of the moral exploitation of soldiers, coupled with the limited neurological and epistemic capacities of most adolescent recruits targeted, gives some non-negligible reason to raise the minimum age of military recruitment for the all-volunteer force. We think the cumulative case gives significant weight to such a position. We take this to be the most obvious "low-hanging fruit" prescription we'd argue for in combating the morally problematic relationship our society finds itself in toward its military. This is not, of course, to infantilize recruits, only to point out that both the state and society grant the relevance of age in other moral contexts (i.e., driving, marriage, sex, alcohol consumption, voting, etc.). It seems plausible then that this thinking should carry over into the space of killing and breaking things on behalf of the nation. Accordingly, we suggest that the minimum age of recruitment be raised to somewhere to (at least) around twenty or twenty-one years of age, or that there be an institutional distinction allowing for recruitment for national defense purposes for younger recruits versus service in primarily expeditionary capacities for older recruits.

Demographic Targeting
With respect to demographic targeting, as noted, the recruitment data clearly reflects an overwhelming demographic target

skewing toward a thin sliver of American society based on class, region, age, and family lineage. The recruitment demographic data demonstrates that the lion's share of physical and moral burdens reflects a lopsided distribution of the duty of civic defense, as well as its concomitant moral responsibilities, toward primarily rural, southern, working-class men, and members of military families. Given this lopsided distribution, we argue that recruitment for military service should be deliberately tipped toward a wider set of demographic targeting across the overall demos.

Recruitment Content
One could argue that this is the easiest of our claims to substantiate—and we'd agree—but we conclude with prejudice that the actual content of military recruitment should be changed to more accurately reflect both the upsides and downsides of the profession of arms, both morally and pragmatically speaking. This would then include changes to recruitment content that involve not merely better acknowledgment of potential physical harms that might be incurred during service but also the *moral* burdens and potential "dirty hands" scenarios that one might encounter while acting in service to the nation. If a citizen has a duty to their country in terms of its defense, then it seems only fair that a country's government should be minimally transparent about the actual specifics of what that duty might entail, not just in terms of physical risk but also moral burdens. Otherwise, if the recruitment content remains as it stands now—largely a set of monetary, educational, and job skill incentives, dressed up in patriotic garb, with acknowledgment of physical risk, but with no acknowledgment of moral risk whatsoever—then the present recruitment arrangement amounts to a form of false advertising or bait-and-switch. The phrase *caveat emptor*, or "buyer beware," might be wholly appropriate for a transaction between customers and businesses on the free market, but what we are talking about here—an appeal to duty to defend

one's country—is not the kind of thing amenable to a mere transactional exchange like a regular commodity such as a stock option or a dishwasher.

Note well: This is, arguably, the same reasoning behind why some Navy SEALs have recently voiced discomfort and concern over the increasing "Branding of the Trident" on the commercial market and in advertising.[2] Further, the nature and telos of the state, as well as its concomitant duties and special relationship to its citizens, especially its young citizens, are arguably different in kind from just any old private business entity relating to customers or employees. This would then imply that the state would be failing in one of its duties to its citizens if, to quote Goodin, it "played for advantage" against a small and arguably vulnerable segment of its young citizens by failing to accurately represent the physical and moral content entailed in the recruitment agreement. This brings us to the larger societal question: If it is natural for a citizen to feel obligated (or even have desire) to defend his or her home, family, and country, then why does the present state require that such cunning, expensive, and manipulative recruitment practices be employed upon its young citizenry? It would seem there is a disconnect between the present practices of recruitment and the supposed civic virtues they claim to trade in. If there is the latter and they are decisive, as is the claim, then why do we need the former? We do not.

---

[2] See Forest Crowell, "Seals Gone Wild: Publicity, Fame, and the Loss of the Quiet Professional" (MA Thesis, Naval Postgraduate School, 2015), https://calhoun.nps.edu/handle/10945/47927. Also see, Nicholas Kulish, Christopher Drew, and Sean Naylor, "Rift Among Navy SEALs Over Members Who Cash In on Brand," *New York Times*, April 2, 2016, https://www.nytimes.com/2016/04/03/us/navy-seals-split-over-members-benefiting-from-hard-earned-brand.html. Duty, like service, trust, friendship, comradery, honor, love, art, beauty, virtue, dignity, merit, meaning, and the sacred, just doesn't seem to be *the kind of good* that can just be traded or bought and sold in a free-market exchange without *the very act of buying and selling* rendering the very nature of that good into something else entirely, thereby destroying its constitutive essence. For instance, *paying someone* to be your friend destroys the very essence of friendship.

Compensation Reform

The moral exploitation of soldiers also motivates the need for institutional reform with respect to active-duty soldier and veteran compensation. Indeed, present compensation for both active-duty soldiers and veterans, in many ways, mirrors the present recruitment relationship, in that both recruitment and compensation significantly ameliorate and paper over the drastically lopsided division of moral labor occurring beneath the surface between the soldier and civilian society. Hence, shallow compensatory gestures, like yellow ribbons on the backs of automobiles, military-appreciation days at the waterpark, Applebees 10% Off-All-You-Can-Eat Veteran's Discounts, and the ubiquitous and near maddening phrase for many veterans of "Thank You for Your Service," all amount to a kind of performative theater within mainstream society failing to grip anything real, or meaningful, or substantive. The felt shallowness and poverty of these now all-too-common social performances hint at an underlying moral landscape inadequately attended to and lacking proper expression for some time now. This, however, is slowly changing, and there are, in fact, several social initiatives and grassroots movements throughout the country, while still in their infancy, that we believe constitute a substantively different kind of relationship between soldier and civilian. Specifically, initiatives like Sebastian Junger and Congressman Seth Molten's Veteran Townhall, and the Theater of War Project, exemplify the kind of platforms and projects we believe could help close the civil-military divide and allow for a more authentic relationship between soldiers, veterans, and civilians.[3] Such initiatives give new avenues for veterans to voice and express themselves without dialogue being forced into the hackneyed default stereotypes of either

---

[3] See John Muldoon, "Moulton to Host Veterans' Town Hall on Veterans' Day," *Ipswich Local News,* November 2, 2020, http://thelocalne.ws/2020/11/02/moulton-hosts-veterans-town-hall-on-veterans-day/.

"veteran as victim" or conversely, "veteran as unreproachable hero." Such initiatives also give spaces where soldiers and veterans can choose to talk or not talk, share or not, without it becoming a melodramatic cryfest antithetical to the warrior ethos. If government spending is to be allotted for better veteran compensation, we argue that it should prioritize these types of initiatives. These are efforts that, in essence, give veterans a means, forum, and permission to engage in a more dialogical, artistic, expressive, and representative space in civic life.

Prudential and Moral Considerations

These suggested reforms in the areas of recruitment and compensation would likely entail certain upsides and downsides both prudentially and morally speaking. In terms of recruitment reform, one obvious upside would be that the state and wider American society wouldn't be morally exploiting its younger citizens so much. In such a state of affairs, the all-volunteer force could then be said, surprisingly, to be *actually* volunteer. And this would arguably be a prima facie good.

The pragmatic downside of such a policy, however, would be the danger of America being unable to field an effective standing, professional fighting force and thus possibly compromising defense of its national borders and international standing as *the* global superpower and leader of the free world. This is an increasingly overdue conversation that the American public, particularly the millennial generation, must have among its civilians, soldiers, veterans, statesmen, and citizens.[4] We will speak more on this shortly.

Even with such reforms in military recruitment and compensation, however, one might still worry that, in the long run, such

---

[4] Bacevich, for instance, intimates that America should return to a quasi-isolationist posture, at least for a while.

prescriptions attend only to symptoms and not root causes. Indeed, one might argue that, such reforms if implemented, would actually make things *worse* overall insofar as they would further prolong and likely widen and exacerbate the existing civil-military divide and its accompanying lopsided division of moral labor. Indeed, even with the implementation of such suggested reforms, it would nonetheless remain true that the moral burdens of America's warfighting and foreign policy efforts would still continue to be shouldered by the same 1% of the American population (and, in truth, an even thinner sliver of that) on behalf of the decisions of the other 99%, who remained otherwise physically, epistemically, and morally sheltered from the actual consequences of their collective decision-making.

As Bacevich and other scholars have noted, the presence of a standing, professional force significantly increases the likelihood of overuse and adventurism by functioning as an expedient foreign policy tool for leaders to quickly and frequently reach to in lieu of less violent, diplomatic means and methods. With a radically detached civilian demos who is both socially and epistemically quarantined from the day-to-day effects of their nation's warfighting actions (barring civilians in military towns), there is a real danger, so the argument goes, of there being no real reason or incentive for such a demos to sincerely care. As one company grade officer noted during the 2003 invasion of Iraq, "if Little League Baseball is still going on in Fayetteville, North Carolina, then America is not *really* at war."[5] Hence, if the bulk of the civilian demos is not seeing, witnessing, and feeling on a visceral and immediate level, the day-to-day impact and second-order effects of their nation's military conflicts (i.e., parents disappearing from their communities, social fabric deteriorating, friends and loved ones returning in coffins, etc.), then it is only human nature that the bulk of civic attention

---

[5] Note to the nonmilitary reader that Fayetteville, NC, is right next to Ft. Bragg, the Army's largest military installation.

will prioritize some other concern, be it moral, nonmoral, prudential, or simply the shiniest new distraction.

Indeed, this danger, of a too-wide civil-military divide was the
reason that, during the initial foundation of the all-volunteer force
after Vietnam, (then) Secretary of Defense General Creighton
Abrams insisted that deployment of US active-duty forces during
wartime legally required the concurrent mobilization of the US
National Guard.[6] This provision, thin as it might have been, at least
still had the wisdom and foresight to institutionally tether the civilian demos to the professional military force in some meaningful
and palpable way such that the divide did not become too wide.

A final contingent moral worry of the present civil-military divide
is that it is not a static gap; rather, it is a dynamic pair of diverging
azimuths, growing wider and further apart over each succeeding generation. America's history over the last hundred years seems to bear
out this trend of increased civil-military widening; from the mobilization of whole townships of citizen-soldiers in World War I and
World War II, to employment of a draft model during Vietnam, to a
shift to the 1% all-volunteer force post-Vietnam, to present-day "gray
zone" conflicts fought across the world almost exclusively by means of
Special Forces operators and drone pilots.

One might wonder where such an institutional direction of travel
is ultimately taking us if left unabated. Will the next generation of
America's warfighters be made up of a set of elite, bio-enhanced,
body-cammed Super Spartans controlled from afar by joysticks in
the hands of a civilian demos resembling characters from the movie
Wall-E? Or the formation of a new 1% warrior/martyr caste whose
primary role is to function as a container of sorts to absorb the physical and moral consequences of the foreign policy decisions of a
collective of political indoor cats? Or perhaps a *1984*-type dystopia

---

[6] See Miranda Summers Lowe, "The Gradual Shift to an Operational Reserve,"
Military Review: The Professional Journal of the U.S. Army, May-June 2019, https://www.
armyupress.army.mil/Journals/Military-Review/English-Edition-Archives/May-June-
2019/Summers-Lowe-Reserve-1990s/.

where the hum of the Forever War is pushed even further into the background of the social imagination as its pragmatic and moral effects are shouldered by a chosen set of individuals shrinking evermore in number and growing evermore invisible within society at large? These questions may sound outside of the realm of possibility at present, but so did the present state of affairs to many just but a few decades ago.

Reflection on these questions motivates one to wonder how far such a widening can be practically and permissibly pushed. One might also worry what detriment to character such an institutional direction of travel could engender for both sides, especially for civilians. If one believes it is a prima facie good for one's character development that persons actually shoulder moral responsibilities or that the virtues of courage, self-sacrifice, stoicism, self-reliance, and resilience (what William James referred to as the "martial virtues") are similarly good for people to cultivate, then the all-volunteer model effectively robs 99% of the population from contexts, opportunities, and experiences whereby such virtues could begin to find proper expression and cultivation.[7] Lastly, it is a general fact of human nature that people, by and large, want to feel useful instead of useless. The present civil-military arrangement, one could argue, perhaps robs many members of the civilian demos from the opportunity to feel and be useful to the society that they care about and are a part of—or so one could conclude given the decayed state of civic involvement for so many. Such a state of affairs is thereby in fact (arguably) detrimental to the character of many civilians insofar as it might foster a kind of perpetual civic adolescence of sorts, a general lack of appreciation for "the small things" in domestic life, or a lack of gratitude for the sacrifices of one's fellow citizens or one's forebearers. To then have future foreign policy

[7] William, James, "The Moral Equivalent of War," *Popular Science Monthly* 77 (October 1910): 400–12. For more, see Marilyn Fischer, "'The Moral Equivalent of War': William James's Minor Variation on Common Themes," *William James Studies* 14, no. 1 (Spring 2018): 92–119.

leadership decisions emerge from such ranks seems increasingly imprudent, if not negligent.

Conversely, one might also worry about the detriment to character that such an institutional scheme might create for members of the all-volunteer force, be it active duty, reservist, or veteran. Within active-duty and reservist ranks, the present civil-military scheme might begin to foster a general antipathy toward civilians who arguably excessively benefit from their physical and moral sacrifices.[8] Such a scheme might also engender what amounts to a growing resentment within some soldiers for the myriad academicians, bureaucrats, policymakers, lawmakers, agencies, subagencies, sub-sub-agencies, and so on who keep disseminating new contradictory rules, regulations, and restrictions at an increasing rate while being comfortably distanced from the real-world implications of such speech that soldiers will inevitably have to sort through on the ground.[9] In combat we might then worry that such a Babel-like institutional network of rules, protocols, directives, rules of engagement, and so forth could lead some soldiers to fatalistically throw up their hands in a moment of frustration or duress and conclude, "If everything I do will be wrong, then why constrain myself at all?" This is clearly not the attitude we want frontline soldiers fighting on behalf of our collective demos to arrive at.

Conversely, it is equally foolhardy and likely morally wrong to continue to send only a small sliver of our overall population into increasingly risky and increasingly morally ambiguous combat contexts and to then demand that they be simultaneously optimally effective warriors and moral saints, both Achilles and Mother

---

[8] This is, in many ways, the book's main thesis.

[9] We may liken this somewhat to a group of pure mathematicians relying upon theoretical non-Euclidean geometric postulates to inform building designs for civil engineers in the real world. The postulates may, in principle *be correct* in the strictest sense, but they are ultimately impractical if not actually *dangerous* for engineers and construction workers to attempt to implement in reality. Moreover, it is also naive and/or insincere for us to think that such hypothetical academic conjectures and performances *are not* in some real way constituting actual policy prescriptions.

Theresa at the same time, when we ourselves will likely never be in such harrowing scenarios. However, we are arguably moving closer to such a state of affairs on both accounts given the present civil-military scheme.

The present too-wide civil-military divide is also arguably bad for veterans insofar as it provides very few real institutional mechanisms and/or a thick social fabric for them to reintegrate back into even if they earnestly sought to. Such societal regard of its returning warriors would be completely foreign if not wholly unintelligible to earlier cultures like the Apache or city-states like Sparta or Athens who each had sophisticated and meaningful warrior-return rituals and tragic plays functioning as a form of collective atonement, appreciation, reflection, and catharsis for soldiers and civilians alike.[10] What's more, such returning soldiers would thereafter be held in the highest of esteem within such societies, functioning as local leaders in midlife and as wise elders in their later years.[11] As previously noted, nowadays it is bizarrely the case that the Hollywood actor who pretends to be a soldier in a movie will be held in higher social esteem, and lexically so, than the actual soldier that he plays.

Such an alienating divide between civilian and returning soldier would even be equally strange and foreign for someone living in just the first half of the twentieth century. Indeed, could films like *Rambo* or *The Hurt Locker*—movies nearly thirty years apart, yet within this shifting social construct we are trying to frame—be made in a small English town immediately after World War I, where all the men would have deployed and redeployed together back to that very same hometown to process their shared experiences for the remainder of their adult lives? In the first film, the returning soldier brings the war home with him and violently lashes out

---

[10] See Sebastian Junger, *Tribe: On Homecoming and Belonging* (New York, 2016).
[11] Our social neglect of older veterans arguably tracks a general societal disregard for the elderly as well.

against an alien domestic town that he cannot integrate with. In the latter film, the soldier flees from domestic life altogether to return to the battlefield, the only context where things make meaningful sense to him.

As noted, the statistical data and metrics on veteran homelessness, PTSD, moral injury, and the like, all point to American society's general failure to returning servicemen and servicewomen. Needless to say, such depressing data is sadly not at all surprising and indeed symptomatic of what has now become a much larger problem within twenty-first-century mainstream American society; an increasingly thinning, increasingly atomized, and increasingly superficial social fabric—one where we soon needn't care about the ills of homeless veterans, for there will be neither a home for soldiers to redeploy back to nor a home for soldiers to deploy *from* in the first place.

Accordingly, given the increased potential for executive overuse and adventurism; abuse by lobbyists, corporate, and foreign interests; rudderless institutional momentum; civil-military detriment; and a civilian principle who is, for the most part, largely apathetic or even actively against "defense in their name" altogether, there is strong reason for the American demos to consider ending the current all-volunteer model of military service.

Furthermore, this last point, of a radically detached or even actively oppositional segment of the civilian populace, generates not only potential downstream or contingent moral worries related to the all-volunteer force but also a potentially significant in-principle moral problem as well. This in-principle moral problem, perhaps best articulated by Jonathan Parry, can be stated as follows: Since soldiers ostensibly draw their moral justification for warfighting, some at least in part and some quite considerably,[12] from the will of the civilian demos, then such civilian apathy and/or active

---

[12] Certain revisionist views might object to this as being a legitimate or significant justificatory reason.

opposition to such warfighting efforts severely problematizes the soldier's capacity to legitimately draw his or her warfighting justification from this source.[13]

For instance, many civilians, both left-leaning pacifists and right-leaning libertarians alike, say, often take offense to the military's common reference to themselves as "sheepdogs." Minimally, such an analogy is arguably offensive to many civilians insofar as it connotes that civilians are fundamentally defenseless "sheep" incapable of self-defense and therefore in need of perpetual protection. More problematic, and this is Parry's point, is that such an analogy presupposes that civilians have *consented* to such protection on their behalf in the first place and, furthermore, that such protection should take the specific form that it has, that is, a series of ongoing, never-ending, primarily Middle Eastern expeditionary wars and conflicts.[14]

We may liken this relationship between soldier and civilian to the paramedic and the Seventh Day Adventist wearing a bracelet stating, "do not resuscitate under any circumstances." All things being equal, most people would agree that the paramedic has a prima facie duty or hypothetical contract to, under normal conditions, resuscitate someone who has fallen unconscious. However, given the Seventh Day Adventist's preemptive waiving/ intentional overriding of his right to be saved, one would think that the paramedic is then doing something wrong against the Seventh Day Adventist by choosing to disregard such a waiver and resuscitate him anyway.[15]

In this same way, Parry argues, the soldier or military body is doing something wrong against the pacifist who claims "Not in

---

[13] See Jonathan Parry, "War and Moral Consistency," in Hugh LaFollette (ed.), *Ethics in Practice: An Anthology* (Chichester, UK, 2020), 692–703.

[14] For more on the "sheepdog" analogy and some helpful and all too relevant points on this score, see Larry Lengbeyer, "Rhetoric Matters: Inviting Military Overreach with the Sheepdog Analogy," *Journal of Military Ethics* 20, no. 1 (June 2021): 21–46.

[15] Parry, "War and Moral Consistency," 698–9.

My Name" by illegitimately helping themselves to the set of moral reasons (derived from his bodily autonomy/self-ownership) that the pacifist has waived by his own choosing. On Parry's view, the pacifist has removed this particular good from the overall "pot" of moral reasons that the soldier can now legitimately draw for his other defensive justifications.

Clearly the pacifist would be analogous to the Seventh Day Adventist in this example. However, the moral and metaphysical status of the apathetic and epistemically indifferent civilian is not so obvious. Is the apathetic civilian's default moral status like that of the Seventh Day Adventist or not? Put another way, can the soldier or military body help themselves to the moral reasons of a group of civilians who don't care all that much one way or the other about wars allegedly being fought on their behalf? Or does the military body require a positive confirmation from such a group—perhaps in the form of a majority, supermajority, or special referendum?

If a soldier states, "I'm fighting in Country X on your behalf" and the common civilian response is "I do not consent to you fighting on my behalf" or, worse, "What the hell is Country X?," then, morally speaking, the soldier's justification for fighting will necessarily be significantly diminished. Indeed, the soldier can tell himself that he is fighting on their behalf, but fact-relatively speaking, he will likely be no more fighting on their behalf than the paramedic is "helping out" the unconscious Seventh Day Adventist by resuscitating him. Indeed, he might be wronging them. This state of affairs, of a consciously opposing or radically indifferent and uninformed civilian populace, significantly problematizes justification for our present warfighting efforts, at least under our current institutional scheme. This point is particularly poignant in light of Major Utzig's commentary in Chapter 4 regarding the rudderless "bureaucratic inertia" of the war itself and how such bureaucratic and institutional momentum can be oddly causal and self-perpetuating with very few or even no conscious agents behind things at times.

Given this combination of contingent and in-principle moral concerns, one might conclude that all of these related moral and prudential factors are fundamentally emergent features of a now too-wide civil-military divide created, primarily, by the continued existence of the all-volunteer force. If this is the case, then reforms of the kind that we have proposed might actually be painting over, stifling, and/or delaying proper acknowledgment of a more fundamental and important civic fissure. This fissure asks: How far can the moral division of labor between civilian principle and military body be permissibly and pragmatically stretched, even with said reforms being made? How wide can the gap get between defender and defended without it becoming morally perverse?

These rhetorical questions highlight that, in a lot of ways, these suggested reforms and prescriptions are, in essence, merely cosmetic; a moral shifting of chairs on the deck of the *Titanic*, so to speak, while the institutional machinery's overall momentum and direction of travel remains, by and large, the same. To press the analogy further, one might wonder if ethical and pragmatic institutional reform is indeed fully exhausted by such mere chair-shifting or if there are other levels below deck yet to be explored. We believe there is much work desperately needed to be done here. We are cautiously hopeful that perhaps with creative and innovative approaches to how we may yet reconcile this moral quagmire still in serious need of research and discovery, we can find a way toward a greater justice for our society. Setting aside such future hopes for now, let us turn now to entertain several alternative conceptions of civil-military reform.

The Skin in the Game Option

The so-called skin in the game argument, colloquially referred to in military circles, largely argues the following: [16] Without an institutional mechanism intimately connecting national warfighting

---

[16] Large sections of this part of this chapter are taken from Michael Robillard, "Skin the Game," *Journal of Military Ethics*, forthcoming.

and foreign policy decisions to tangible local effects in domestic life, there will be the increased likelihood and tendency for overuse and abuse as well as other probable downstream moral ills.[17] More specifically, such overuse and abuse could take the form of incentivization for adventurism; overuse of the professional force as an expedient foreign policy instrument; overuse by the executive branch; excessive influence by lobbyists, corporatists, big business, and other small party interests (i.e., the military-industrial complex) relative to the will of the demos; uninformed and amateurish leadership at the highest levels of strategy, grand strategy, and statecraft; and a severe and ever-widening civil-military divide within the organs of government and within society at large. Such worries and concerns therefore motivate the idea that the civilian principle and military body ought to be more closely institutionally linked.

Growing Sentiment

Growing sentiment among prominent academic, political, retired military, and journalistic figures has begun to emerge, intimating at some version or another a return to the "skin in the game" model of military service. As noted previously, Vietnam veteran and political scientist, Andrew Bacevich, in his work *Breach of Trust*, advocates a return to a draft or conscription-based model of military service.

---

[17] Similar contingent arguments based on predictive future claims about likelihood of overuse have also been made with respect to emerging military technologies such as semi-autonomous drones and autonomous weapons systems. Among many pieces in the literature discussing this topic, see: Helen Frowe, "The Use of Drones and the Ethics of Defensive Force," 5th Annual Conference of the Oxford Institute for Ethics, Sep 2014. Paul W. Kahn, "The Paradox of Riskless Warfare," *Philosophy and Public Policy Quarterly* 22, no. 3 (2002): 2–9. Robert Sparrow, "Riskless Warfare Revisted: Drones, Asymmetry, and the Just Use of Force," in Christian Enemark (ed.), *Ethics of Drone Strikes: Restraining Remote-Control Killing* (Edinburgh: 2021), 10–30. Bradley J. Strawser, "Moral Predators," *Journal of Military Ethics* 9, no. 4 (December 2010): 342–68. Bradley J. Strawser, Duncan Purves, and Ryan Jenkings, "Autonomous Machines, Moral Judgment, and Acting for the Right Reasons," *Ethical Theory and Moral Practice* 18, no. 4 (August 2015): 851–72. Bradley J. Strawser, *Opposing Perspectives on the Drone Debate* (London: 2014).

Similarly, at a 2012 Aspen Institute Conference, former JSOC Commander, Gen. (ret.) Stanley McChrystal argued for a return to a pre-Vietnam citizen-soldier model of military service. To quote McChrystal:

> I think if a nation goes to war, every town, every city needs to be at risk. . . . You make that decision and everybody has skin in the game.[18]

Lastly, appealing to similar notions of a duty to one's country, journalist and war correspondent Sebastian Junger, in his book *Tribe*, suggests a need for American public life to return to *some* conception of national service, not even necessarily military service for all of its citizens.[19] To quote a 2016 Military.com interview of Junger:

> I think it's a shame that the only way to serve your country is with a gun. I think mandatory national service would throw every component of society into a pot together and stir it up, black, white, poor . . . everybody goes in there. And it would give young people a very valuable lesson that they're actually part of this incredible experiment.[20]

A growing sentiment within the social zeitgeist at large for a desire (or in fact, *need*) for broader civic participation with respect to America's national defense appears to be emerging beyond these

---

[18] Thomas Ricks, "Let's Draft Our Kids," *New York Times*, July 9, 2012, https://www.nytimes.com/2012/07/10/opinion/lets-draft-our-kids.html.

[19] Junger, *Tribe*, 2–3. See also Hope Hodge Seck, "Sebatian Junger's Draft Proposal: Service with Non-Military Options," *Military.com*, June 18, 2016, https://www.military.com/daily-news/2016/06/18/sebastian-junger-draft-proposal-service-with-military-option.html.

[20] Hope Hodge Seck, "Sebatian Junger's Draft Proposal: Service with Non-Military Options," *Military.com*, June 18, 2016, https://www.military.com/daily-news/2016/06/18/sebastian-junger-draft-proposal-service-with-military-option.html.

pockets. For instance, recent political debates and discussions surrounding the need for American women to be legally required to sign up for selective service at the age of eighteen seems to intimate, or, at the very least for some, it begins to symbolically gesture toward this felt sense of moral lopsidedness with respect to equitable distribution of national defense responsibilities. Further still, the fast and growing popularity of millennial-generation veteran congressional representatives such as Dan Crenshaw (TX-R), Seth Molten (MA-D), and Tulsi Gabbard (HI-D), for the most notable examples, similarly suggests a growing respect and acknowledgment in the broader American social consciousness for the gravitas of veteran insights on both domestic and foreign policy issues.

Finally on this point, as noted earlier, a shift to a draft or national service model of some sort might also be good for the character and overall psyche of many American civilians, particularly for restless young men in society, in want of a deeper sense of purpose, meaning, and vocation. Setting aside what one may think of their peculiar politics, some interesting examples of this—at least anthropomorphically—might be found where we see the "signal strength" of this issue in the surprising rise of those commentators who explicitly call for undertaking communal responsibility, even at expense of oneself. The meteoric rise of Canadian psychologist Jordan Peterson and (perhaps surprising) receptiveness to his prescription for young, directionless men to "find a heavy responsibility, pick it up, and then carry it!" suggests an underlying yearning in large segments of North American society for something more metaphysically robust and substantial than the latest new consumer product, creature comfort, or hedonic distraction.[21] Again, set

---

[21] Institutionally and pragmatically speaking, this might look like a draft or conscription-based model, a mandatory active military service model, mandatory national-guard model, a nonmilitary national service model, or some hybridized version of all of these elements. Several presently existing templates for national service can be found in Israel, South Korea, and Switzerland. Minimally speaking, a "war tax" might be another sort of institutional mechanism to yoke military actions with domestic consequences and sacrifice.

aside the politics of Peterson and the like. The eager response—especially from young people, and especially young men of so-called fighting age, makes one pause—and is in wont of explanation.

Prudential and Moral Considerations

There are, of course, several considerable upsides and downsides to the idea of American society rolling things back to a pre-Vietnam style citizen-soldier model of national military service or to something like it. In terms of upsides, some of the goods of a draft or national service model we have briefly touched on. Some of these major upsides might include a more equitable sharing of the overall moral and nonmoral burdens of America's warfighting, foreign policy, and national defense decisions; a closing of the civil-military gap within official organs of government and within greater society; less likelihood of abuse or overuse of the military by the executive branch or by other small group interests; a republic more in line with the tenets and spirit originally laid out in the Constitution; and a drawdown of the ongoing "Forever War" of expeditionary projects, primarily those in the Middle East.

There are also several obvious and not so obvious downsides to such a drastic and sudden shift in civil-military relations. Domestically speaking, such a shift could generate possible riots or pockets of civil unrest not unlike the protests to the Vietnam War seen in the 1960s with respect to instituting the draft.[22] Also with respect to overall national defense and world dominance, there is the worry that a citizen-soldier model of military service could lead over time to an amateurish force and therefore result in a diminishing of America's global superpower reputation. The consequence of this potential diminishing could also

---

[22] Ironically, in this case we would be suggesting a draft as a mechanism to *end* our ongoing wars not as a mechanism to bolster a war that we had just begun.

generate potentially pernicious downstream effects in the form of weakened national defense capabilities, unfinished Middle Eastern projects, and failures to quickly and successfully respond in an interventionist capacity to future human rights violations around the world.

All this being said, it is important we are not too quick to conflate the fielding of an all-volunteer force with America necessarily taking the role of a cosmopolitan or interventionist world policeman, or, conversely, we do not conflate a conscription or draft-based military service model with a strict isolationist foreign policy posture. Indeed, independent of whether America's future foreign policy posture tends to be more interventionist or isolationist in nature, our main point still holds: The moral responsibility for such military actions needs to be more evenly distributed among the American public at large. Accordingly, we positively advocate for a return to the skin in the game policy option.

The Butler Option

In his famous 1935 work, *War is a Racket*, Major General Smedley Butler, then the most decorated living marine in the US Marine Corps, argued that, upon deep reflection on his military service and the wars he had taken part in in defense of the American people and the American homeland, his efforts had in actuality materially contributed not to America's defense but rather to increasing the profits of big business and war profiteers.[23] Having served in what he later determined to be unjustified US campaigns for the primary interests of the U.S. Fruit Company in the so-called Banana Wars of Central America and the Caribbean (1898–1934), Butler's polemic

---

[23] Smedley Butler, "War Is a Racket," speech delivered on a nation-wide tour in the early 1930s. The speech was eventually turned into a short book: Smedley Butler, *War is a Racket* (San Juan, 1935).

argued for drastic institutional reform to protect against such un-justified influences on future US foreign policy.

In his work, Butler argued for the following set of institutional prescriptions to, as he says, "smash the war racket." He wrote:

1. We must take the profit out of war.
2. We must permit the youth of the land who would bear arms to decide whether or not there should be war.
3. We must limit our military forces to home defense purposes.[24]

With respect to each of these three prescriptions, Butler outlined the following:

Let the officers and the directors and the high-powered executives of our armament factories and our munitions makers and our shipbuilders and our airplane builders and the manufacturers of all the other things that provide profit in war time as well as the bankers and the speculators, be conscripted—to get $30 a month, the same wage as the lads in the trenches get.

Another step necessary in this fight to smash the war racket is the limited plebiscite to determine whether a war should be declared. . . . It would be a simple   matter each year for the men coming of military age to register in their communities as they did in the draft during the World War and be examined physically. Those who could pass and who would therefore be called upon to bear arms in the event of war would be eligible to vote in a limited plebiscite. They should be the ones to have the power to decide—and not a Congress few of whose members are within the age limit and fewer still of whom are in physical condition to bear arms. Only those who must suffer should have the right to vote.

---

[24] Butler, *War Is a Racket.*

> A third step in this business of smashing the war racket is to make certain that our military forces are truly forces for defense only.[25]

While the present composition of the US armed forces, the character of civil-military relations, and the nature of America's current wars are markedly different from the military, society, and wars Butler was specifically responding to in his day and time, the deeper structural considerations underpinning both past and present are nonetheless quite similar. Whereas in Butler's time, the composition of the US military was organized in accordance with a draft-based model and the chief external threat to the United States was perceived to be far more regional and hemispheric in nature, the influence of big business interests on US foreign policy decision-making and the corresponding lack of serious regard for the voices of soldiers and veterans has remained largely constant during present-day US wars and in civil-military relations. Accordingly, on our view, Butler's set of institutional prescriptions, particularly the spirit of his second prescription with respect to soldiers having exclusive voice in warfighting decisions, has strong appeal in its potential to ameliorate the moral exploitation of soldiers that we have here noted. In other words, if the shouldering of excess moral burdens and the excessive bearing of dirty hands on behalf of the demos is not somehow offset by institutional reforms in the form of recruitment and compensation or by a return to a conscription or draft-based model of military service and thereby a *sharing* of warfighting responsibilities, then the only reasonable institutional reform left on the table would seem to be for such dirty hands to translate into corresponding authority, voice, and increased political standing of some sort.[26] As to whether

[25] Butler, *War Is a Racket.*
[26] Some have suggested that our call here would be a kind of "first right of refusal" for the military, as an institution, for any foreign intervention. Thanks to Christopher Kutz for help on this point.

such institutional change should take the specific form of an exclusive plebiscite for military members, as Butler suggests, is uncertain. Indeed, greater and more equitable political representation of soldiers and regard for veteran voices within the official organs of government could be similarly achieved via other institutional and policy prescriptions as well. Specifically, a new provision requiring that a certain minimum number of active Congressmen/women serve or have served within the military, or that their children serve, could arguably achieve a similar effect.[27] So too could a provision requiring that a certain number of active Congressmen/women deploy "down range" and put themselves in harm's way alongside their fellow countrymen for a given stint during their time in office. Such policy prescriptions, though admittedly imperfect, would then at least move us somewhat closer back to the Jeffersonian adage, "Every citizen should be a soldier. This was the case with the Greeks and Romans, and must be that of every free state." And while such policy prescriptions wouldn't require all American citizens to fulfill this role of soldier, such policy reforms would, at the very least, demand skin in the game sacrifices from those at the heights of governmental power who make such influential foreign policy decisions for soldiers and civilians alike. To our minds, this seems only fitting for what American citizens should expect and demand from their freely chosen *leaders*, not just managers.

The Future and Fate of the American Soul

Policy prescriptions and surface-level institutional reforms aside, our greater aim with respect to this book and overall project is for the soul of America to fundamentally change. We don't want Americans to suddenly give more of a damn now, as it were. We

---

[27] This is discussed in the Michael Moore film *Fahrenheit 9/11*.

want them to have given a damn in the first place. And while it is impossible for us to fix such collective apathy in the past, we nonetheless believe that some of the institutional reforms we have suggested could help significantly with respect to curing such civic apathy and disproportionate shouldering of moral responsibility heading into the future. Can this shift in cultural conscience be pragmatically achieved without significant institutional reform of the sorts we have suggested? Or, can such a shift occur perhaps by some other set of reforms or prescriptions we have not imagined or articulated in this book? Indeed, it is too soon to for us say. However, it is abundantly clear by now that some sort of cultural shift is needed and needed soon. For if no shift whatsoever begins to occur within American society, within America's present civil-military relationship, and within America's soul, then this state of affairs as we head further into the twenty-first century will show itself to be not only imprudent, or unsustainable, or unfair, or unjust; indeed, it will show itself to be positively absurd. Accordingly, if no institutional reforms of any of those noted here are achieved or acted upon, then we as Americans should be honest with ourselves and admit what our present civil-military scheme has become and what it now actually is: a warrior caste.

Conclusion

This book has been our attempt to articulate a cluster of related moral and political issues and concepts; some more philosophical, some more practical, centered on what we see as a peculiar, markedly lopsided, and ultimately unfair division of labor between American society and its warfighters. Specifically, we have argued that the division of labor—physical, psychological, and, most importantly, *moral*—that presently exists between the all-volunteer force and the greater American public can best be described as exploitative, both in terms of recruitment practices specifically and civil-military relations more generally. Further, because of the set of moral duties that has been disproportionately and repeatedly outsourced to a very small segment of the American citizenry by a largely apathetic and politically disinterested public, particularly over the last two decades worth of warfighting, we have argued for the strong need for major institutional reforms. Morality demands that we must try to rectify these problems.

The institutional reforms we have here argued for run the gamut from military-specific reforms in the areas of recruitment and compensation, to broader and more sweeping changes in civil-military relations, specifically in the forms of national military service and greater political representation for veterans within the organs of government. It is our view that effective and just warfighting and foreign policy requires, among other things, prudent and ethical decision-making prior to conflict, collective sharing of effort and responsibility during conflict (and hence, increased likelihood of dirty hands), firsthand experiential knowledge and competency,

Outsourcing Duty. Michael J. Robillard and Bradley J. Strawser, Oxford University Press. © Oxford University Press 2022. DOI: 10.1093/oso/9780190671457.003.0007

and collective atonement and reflection thereafter. Such concerns, we argue, moral or otherwise, are only made possible by means of substantive institutional reforms that will drive people in society to care about these things.

Moreover, as we have argued, it is not clear that moral duties of national defense are *in principle* fully and completely alienable and thereby subject to mere transactional exchange in the ways our present recruitment scheme and civil-military division of labor seem to easily assume. Even if they are in principle transferrable in this way, we nonetheless have argued that this transfer has resulted in what has now become a disproportionate and ultimately unfair distribution of moral burdens within American society. Lastly, as a contingent matter, we have argued that the dirty hands of the 1% may no longer even be causally contributing all that much to core American values like defense of the US Constitution, defense of the homeland, or expressive of the collective will of the American demos at large. This last point, about an increasing divergence between collective intention and actual causal effect generates a central question in need of answering for both civilians and soldiers alike: *For whom or what do we fight, not just in word and intention but also in deed and consequence?*

For civilians, this question should generate sober and honest reflection over duties to one's country. For soldiers and veterans, this question should generate reflection over duties of self-regard and contemplation over what one is and has been fighting for in actuality, not in theory or in slogans. And for both, especially with regard to our present and future political leadership, this question should generate serious contemplation regarding America's role and mission in the world and its future trajectory.

What then is the future of America and the fate of the sons and daughters sworn to protect it? Is it to be law enforcers of the emerging neoliberal world order, policemen of cosmopolis? Or is it to bring all the troops home, to put up a shield, build a huge wall, metaphorically or perhaps literally, and adopt a strict isolationist foreign policy? Is there some middle way between such extremes, but born out of principle not milquetoast indifference?

The answering of this question will ultimately be—or, as we have argued, *should* be—a collective decision arrived at through the deliberations of every individual American citizen within this country. Regardless, the 1% of America's citizenry comprising her armed forces, standing silently on that wall separating order from anarchy, will be essential whatever our future foreign policy orientation happens to be. Civilians and veterans alike must ask themselves where their priorities and duties ultimately lie—with respect to the world, to foreign allies, to fellow citizens and countrymen, to community, to family and friends, to self, and . . . to soldiers.

It is important to remember as well that any future foreign policy avenues will require willful cooperation on the part of the warrior caste presently standing on that wall and from those who have served on that wall. Such cooperation and the filling of such future ranks should not be taken lightly or for granted. And it will likely not be as easily achieved as it has been in the past given our civil-military relationship as it presently stands: largely exchanging indulgences for dirty hands, bribery for responsibility, and penance for a clean conscience. The men and women whom we have served with, taught, and loved over the last twenty years and who have served and continue to serve this great country of ours deserve much better. They have carried much more of their share of the moral load for this nation, and it is past the time for the rest of America's citizenry to do the same. A growing awareness within an increasing number of soldiers and veterans alike in this country is fast on the rise; one of fairness, recognition, respect, and *thumos*. Some would call it a kind of awakening; it is, to our minds, a sentiment long overdue at a minimum, and necessary. To quote at length from Kipling's *Tommy*:

> *I went into a public-'ouse to get a pint o' beer,*
> *The publican 'e up an' sez, "We serve no red-coats here."*

The girls be'ind the bar they laughed an' giggled fit to die,
I outs into the street again an' to myself sez I:
O it's Tommy this, an' Tommy that, an' "Tommy, go away";
But it's "Thank you, Mister Atkins," when the band begins to play,
The band begins to play, my boys, the band begins to play,
O it's "Thank you, Mister Atkins," when the band begins to play.

I went into a theatre as sober as could be,
They gave a drunk civilian room, but 'adn't none for me;
They sent me to the gallery or round the music-'alls,
But when it comes to fightin', Lord! they'll shove me in the stalls!
For it's Tommy this, an' Tommy that, an' "Tommy, wait outside";
But it's "Special train for Atkins" when the trooper's on the tide,
The troopship's on the tide, my boys, the troopship's on the tide,
O it's "Special train for Atkins" when the trooper's on the tide.

Yes, makin' mock o' uniforms that guard you while you sleep
Is cheaper than them uniforms, an' they're starvation cheap;
An' hustlin' drunken soldiers when they're goin' large a bit
Is five times better business than paradin' in full kit.
Then it's Tommy this, an' Tommy that, an' "Tommy, 'ow's yer soul?"
But it's "Thin red line of 'eroes" when the drums begin to roll,
The drums begin to roll, my boys, the drums begin to roll,
O it's "Thin red line of 'eroes" when the drums begin to roll.

We aren't no thin red 'eroes, nor we aren't no blackguards too,
But single men in barricks, most remarkable like you;
An' if sometimes our conduck isn't all your fancy paints,
Why, single men in barricks don't grow into plaster saints;
While it's Tommy this, an' Tommy that, an' "Tommy, fall be'ind,"
But it's "Please to walk in front, sir," when there's trouble in the
   wind,
There's trouble in the wind, my boys, there's trouble in the wind,
O it's "Please to walk in front, sir," when there's trouble in the wind.

You talk o' better food for us, an' schools, an' fires, an' all:
We'll wait for extry rations if you treat us rational.
Don't mess about the cook-room slops, but prove it to our face
The Widow's Uniform is not the soldier-man's disgrace.
For it's Tommy this, an' Tommy that, an' "Chuck him out, the
brute!"
But it's "Saviour of 'is country" when the guns begin to shoot;
An' it's Tommy this, an' Tommy that, an' anything you please;
An' Tommy ain't a bloomin' fool—you bet that Tommy sees![1]

. . . You bet that Tommy sees.

[1] Rudyard Kipling, "Tommy" in *Barrack-Room Ballads* (Philadelphia, 1930): 6–7.

Epilogue

Cheyney Ryan

> *As soldiers are reasonable beings, as such they are to be*
> *treated.*
> —Thomas Pickering, "Easy Plan for a Militia" (1775)

The image of the soldier has long held a privileged place in American society. For the founders of the United States, it exemplified the stark contrast between corrupt European monarchies, endlessly at war with one another and the world generally, and the new American republic that they sought to create—one that they hoped would be a "peace nation." The armies of the corrupt monarchies were composed of the socially marginalized, compelled to military service from lack of other options, or outright mercenaries. The British soldiers that fought against the American colonists were so much a class apart that many did not even come from Britain, 40 percent of them hired Hessians bound to unlimited military servitude. They constituted a full-time professional "standing army" at the center of the "permanent military establishments" that America's founders feared as the source of tyranny at home and ongoing wars abroad. By contrast, American wars would be fought by "citizen-soldiers" like the "embattled farmer" celebrated in the most famous poem about the American Revolution, Ralph Waldo Emerson's "Concord Hymn." They would not fight because they had no other options or were paid to do so but because they cherished the liberties of a free society; nor would they constitute a class apart—service to one's country in times of need was expected from everyone capable of providing it. Thomas Pickering termed it an "army of equals," whose defining feature was that soldiers "must be clearly informed of the reason of every action and movement and the uses to which they can be applied." Benjamin Franklin had the contrast in mind when he wrote, soon after the Revolution:

> It has been for some time a generally received opinion, that a military man is not to inquire whether a war be just or unjust; he is to execute his orders. All princes who are disposed to become tyrants must probably approve of this opinion, and be willing to establish it; but is it not a dangerous one? Since, on that principle, if the tyrant commands his army to attack and destroy not only an unoffending neighbor nation, but even his own subjects, the army is bound to obey. A Negro slave in our colonies, being commanded by his master to rob and murder a neighbor, or do any other immoral act, may refuse, and the magistrate will protect him in his refusal. The slavery, then, of a soldier is worse than that of a Negro![1]

The soldiers of a republic are free rational agents, not mindless automatons who must do what they're told either from outright compulsion or a corrupt sense of "duty".[2]

Thomas Paine termed this an "army of principles." It has been a hard ideal to realize given, among other things, its obvious tension with the imperatives of military discipline. Baron von Steuben, the man most responsible for instilling discipline into the Continental Army and whose Regulations for the Order and Discipline of the

---

[1] "On the Criminal Laws and the Practice of Privateering," Letter to Benjamin Vaughan, March 14, 1785.

[2] Kant, writing from a republican perspective, is equally critical of treating soldiers as less than autonomous agents. In his 1784 essay, "What Is Enlightenment?," he writes: "But now I hear shouting on all sides! The officer says, 'Don't argue, just drill!' The tax bureau says, 'Don't argue, just pay!' The clergyman says, 'Don't argue just believe!'" For Kant, enlightenment was the emergence from such "dependency," by which he meant the inability to use one's intellect without the supervision of others. ("Dependency" here translates Kant's key term *Unmündigkeit* and *unmündig* that literally mean "mouthless," i.e., "not being able to speak [for oneself].")

Troops of the United States became the Army's drill manual for decades, complained to General George Washington that you could not fight a war if soldiers could argue about every order they were given. And the authors of the US Constitution determined that the security needs of the new republic required that there be a minimal military establishment with full-time officers, subsequently drawn from the military academy established by President Thomas Jefferson. Yet the "citizen-soldier" ideal remained a vital one that continued to inform how the United States fought its wars. For example, when President Woodrow Wilson introduced conscription to fight World War I, he did so by creating an institution—the Selective Service System—that was highly decentralized and staffed by civilians, in keeping with America's traditional suspicion of military establishments and its belief that, if wars must be fought, it must be done by ordinary citizens acting from a sense of civic duty.

What is the fate of the American soldier today? And how does it speak to the larger political issues raised by soldiering that America's founders saw as so vital to what their society was all about?

This is the question Michael Robillard and Bradley Strawser have posed in their important, indeed profound, book. Their work is an important contribution to the ongoing discussions of just war theory; it stands with other recent works in expanding the concerns of that theory—in this case, from questions of what soldiers *do* to questions of who soldiers *are*. But it also raises questions for the citizenry as a whole, in keeping with the deep concern of many public voices today about the place of the military in American life today, as related to the role of the American military in the world generally.

They begin with a note of alarm. "Something is very wrong" they write, focusing on the experience of today's soldiers. On the one hand, soldiers are profusely "thanked for their service" in ways that can verge on the "garish." On the other hand, the average Americans who "thank" them for their service evidence no interest in who soldiers actually are or what soldiers actually do. Their gratitude claims to be heartfelt, but it is more like the gratuity that a customer leaves to a faceless "server," happy that someone else is doing the dirty work. And the academy is not spared from the author's criticism. Fighting for one's country is the most serious civic obligation one can assume. It is one of the only obligations that can permanently alter the trajectory of your life in part because it is the only obligation that can involve intentional killing and dying. So one would think that the ethical questions it raises would be central to political philosophy. But in fact they are invisible. There are extensive discussions around such burning questions as whether Malibu beach surfers have a "right to be fed." Meanwhile the right of the ordinary soldier to be heard goes ignored. In the field of philosophy, there are more articles on what it's like to be a bat than what it's like to be a soldier. What the authors call the "moral experience of soldiering" goes unaddressed—perhaps because the average academic can more easily imagine themselves surfing in Malibu than serving as one of the more than 160,000 American soldiers now stationed in 150 countries overseas.

The authors speak of the relation of the ordinary citizen to the soldier as one of "alienation." I have elsewhere used the term *alienated war* to describe this detachment.[3] It is important to note how recent it is, given how contrary it seems to be to the close connection of citizenship and soldiering in the American founders' citizen-soldier ideal. The turning point was the end of conscription in the early 1970s, an event I would now identify as one of the most significant political changes in my lifetime. Prior to that, military service was something every young man expected to face. Soldiering was not some exotic activity engaged in by an exceptional few, who were effusively "thanked" for so doing. It was a civic duty, and a rather prosaic one at that—like paying one's taxes

[3] See my *The Chickenhawk Syndrome: War, Sacrifice, and Personal Responsibility* (Washington, DC, 2009).

(for which no one needed to be "thanked"). Discussions of conscription today start with acknowledging its inconceivability; calls for reviving the draft are political suicide. How striking it is to note, then, that into the mid-1960s the draft was the most highly esteemed public institution in America, followed closely by the post office. The reason was simple and hearkened back to the vision of America's founders. Serving one's country was what it *meant* to be an "American." This is why the debate over any conscription was such a significant one for it involved the most fundamental issues of national identity.

But now we stand on the other side of the political divide, where a president of the United States can proclaim himself the champion of all things "American" while bragging about avoiding military service and evading paying his taxes. In the words of our authors, something is indeed very wrong. Others have bemoaned the alienation of soldiers from the citizenry. The powerful and strikingly original claim of *Outsourcing Duty* is that the disproportionate moral responsibility imposed on a relatively few soldiers, many of them drawn from more vulnerable groups, constitutes a form of "moral exploitation." It is a striking claim because it is not easily ignored. I think that many ordinary citizens will readily acknowledge a degree of unfairness in who serves in the military but regard it as a matter of no particular urgency. But the upshot of *Outsourcing Duty* is that things cannot be left there. If soldiers are morally exploited, then the ordinary citizen is a moral freeloader or moral parasite. This resonates with the classical civic republican concern with "corruption." And it fits with the passionate concern with personal responsibility that I find animating every page of this book.

We should not idealize the past. The citizen-soldier model had its very great downside in associating patriotism with bellicosity. Conscription was fairer than what we have now, but it was coercive in ways society now finds unacceptable. Conscription was ended in the United States as a response to the Vietnam War and the social conflicts it generated. But it reflected a much larger trend of ending

conscription in Western societies generally.[4] Sir Michael Howard
has portrayed this as the end of "nationalized" war, that is, the in-
tegration of war into society that characterize the two world wars,
and the emergence of "post-nationalized" war, that is, the segrega-
tion of war from society that we see today.[5] A vast literature now
speaks to the dramatic social consequences of this change. But it
remains largely unnoticed by moral and political philosophers
who often speak as if "soldiers" and "militaries" and "war" itself
were some sort of natural kinds, consistent across the millennia
and posing the same problems. *Outsourcing Duty* demands that we
confront the moral challenges posed by soldiering as it is actually
conducted today, by starting with the actual experience of soldiers.

Where do we go next?

The authors conclude with verses by Rudyard Kipling responding
to the soldiers' fate with a note of defiance. The poem "Tommy"
was composed in 1890 and notes that soldiers will tolerate much "if
you treat us rational." Kipling's voice would acquire a note of grief
after his own son's death in World War I, occasioning the famous
lines (from "The Common Form" 1916): "If any questions / why
we died, / Tell them, / because our fathers lied." (The "fathers" here
are national leaders oblivious to the fate of the ordinary soldier.)
The authors are clear about the magnitude of the change required.
It means nothing less than that "the soul of America to fundamentally change." But they are undecided in their specific policy
prescriptions. I find this understandable. If in fact we are still living
in the dawn of "post-nationalized" war, then all of it is very much
up for grabs. But I also find their uncertainty to be appropriate
given their task as political philosophers. The challenge today is
not that policymakers provide the wrong solutions to the problems.

---

[4] See the discussion of this in James J. Sheehan, *Where Have All the Soldiers Gone?: The Transformation of Modern Europe* (Boston, 2009).

[5] See his "War and the Nation-State", *Daedalus* 108, no. 4, The State (Fall, 1979), 101–110.

The challenge is that the nature of the problem is being ignored, specifically the very great ethical problems posed by today's construction of soldiering. It is the achievement of Michael Robillard and Bradley Strawser's *Outsourcing Duty* to bring these into focus, and for that we can all be grateful.

APPENDIX

Criticisms, Questions, and Replies

We were at war while the rest of America was at the mall.
—U.S. Serviceman, circa 2003

Having outlined our general concept of moral exploitation and having made the specific case for the moral exploitation of the American soldier, in this Appendix we will address some common criticisms and questions relating to these areas. Broadly speaking, these criticisms and questions parse into three major types:

1. broad objections concerning exploitation in general,
2. criticisms and concerns regarding our specific concept of moral exploitation, and
3. questions and objections related to the moral exploitation of soldiers.

Let us address each of these in kind.

1. Exploitation

Criticism A: Exploitation is prima facie wrong, however the overall moral weight of exploitation is, all things considered, quite minimal relative to other kinds of wrongs.

Response A:
This claim may or may not be true depending on our background theory of human well-being and whether we are talking about singular exploitative transactions or ongoing exploitative relationships. We believe that it is at least conceivable that a singular exploitative transaction or certainly an ongoing exploitative relationship such as the present institutional relationship between civilians and soldiers could render a person on balance worse off than a case of coercion, oppression, or certain rights violations for instance.

Criticism B: As you note about Matt Zwolinski's challenge, mere neglect is, all things considered, morally worse than exploitation since any exploitative exchange necessarily increases the set of options a vulnerable party possesses prior to the exploitative offer. Hence, sweatshops (or militaries) that exploitatively recruit vulnerable persons actually do something morally less wrong than institutional arrangements that neglect vulnerable persons entirely and offer them no options at all.

Response B:

Even if we grant that objective well-being considerations can be trumped by strong autonomy considerations (or do not factor into the moral equation at all), we believe we can still fully take Zwolinski's point on board. This is so since Zwolinski's argument focuses only on cases involving *adult agents* operating in the *free market* while our argument fundamentally concerns the relationship between *non-adult citizens'* and *the state*, as well as the state's appeals to civic *duty* as part of its advertisement campaign. Insofar as young people don't have the degree of autonomy or knowledge to make fully informed, rational decisions about moral responsibilities endemic to warfighting (to include ad bellum considerations) and insofar as the state ostensibly bears some sort of special duty to not exploit its young citizens, a duty ostensibly absent or at least significantly lessened in free-market exchanges, we believe our thesis of the moral exploitation of American soldiers remains relatively immune from this particular criticism.

2. Moral Exploitation

Criticism C: What if the agent simply wants to take on additional moral responsibility? If the agent, of his or her own accord, simply wants to be the one who shoulders additional moral responsibility, then in such cases, it appears no harm is being done to this agent. In the absence of any harm, there is no wrong here. [1]

Response C:

If this is a problem, then it is not a problem for the concept of moral exploitation exclusively. Indeed, any theory of exploitation, and arguably any theory of oppression as well, will have to deal with these tricky cases where there is a sharp contrast between what appears to be an objective wrong being done to an agent and that agent's own subjective desire for that apparent wrong to be done to him. Indeed, the literature on exploitation takes consensual cases— and ones of mutual all-things-considered benefit—to be the paradigm cases for analysis since these cases of exploitation cannot be explained in terms of

---

[1] We thank Peter Singer for being the first to offer this objection.

other wrongs (e.g., like rights violations). How one finally comes down on this issue will largely depend on his or her background commitments to related concepts such as autonomy as well as subjective versus objective notions of well-being. A full and thorough treatment of these concepts, however, goes well beyond the scope of this book and arguably warrants a book of its own. Suffice it to say, insofar as the concept of moral exploitation is parasitic upon theories of exploitation in general, we do not see Singer's objection as a defeater specific to our particular view. (Note also that our more fleshed out views on supererogation and its relation to moral exploitation can also be found in Chapter 2.)[2]

Criticism D: What's wrong with exposing people to increased moral risk?

Response D:

To play devil's advocate, imagine the case of an intoxicated surgeon who performs surgery drunk but miraculously pulls off the surgery without harming his patient whatsoever. While the surgeon does not harm the patient, it seems as if he still wrongs the patient by exposing her to such needless physical risk. While it may be the case that we wrong someone by exposing that person to the physical risk of an intoxicated surgeon, it does not follow (so the argument goes) that we do the same when we expose that same person to risky moral situations and moral dilemmas where there is an increased risk of *they themselves* making a moral mistake. In the case of the surgery, the potential harm that we expose the victim to is one in which, if it eventuates, the victim will be wholly non-culpable. Conversely, if we expose someone to a difficult moral decision, and he chooses the immoral course of action, then we have arguably done nothing wrong to him whatsoever. Rather, all that we have done is provided him with an opportunity to demonstrate his own lack of character, one which had remained previously hidden merely on account of good moral luck up until that point. At most, it would seem, we have given him an opportunity to wrong himself. If, however, he is a decent person, then, one might further argue, he will make the right choice and will therefore have nothing to worry about.

This line of reasoning would work were it not for the fact that morality and the world in general do not behave so easily. Sometimes an agent with the most impeccable character can still do everything right and nonetheless end up committing wrong. This would hold true for cases of genuine moral dilemmas (where two values are incommensurably at odds with one another) as well as in cases where a pro tanto wrong must be committed for the sake of some all-things-considered good as previously alluded to. In both scenarios,

---

[2] Original articulation of this response can be found in our article, Michael Robillard and Bradley J. Strawser, "On the Moral Exploitation of Soldiers," *Public Affairs Quarterly* (2016), 173–5.

for the decent moral agent, much psychological hardship will likely accompany his moral deliberation. In other words, these will not be easy, stress-free decisions. Therefore, *even if the agent makes all the right decisions* for all the difficult moral challenges thrown at him, it is unlikely that deliberation regarding these issues will be completely stress free nor will it be the case there will be no residual doubt, guilt, or self-blame after the decision has been made. In all likelihood, he will expend some degree of psychological energy after the fact, wondering if his decisions were indeed the correct ones. This is presumably what we find so repugnant about the infamous Milgram experiments.

Thus, it seems as if agents can in fact be wronged simply by having difficult moral decisions thrust upon them, both in terms of the generation of psychological duress (both pre- and post-decision) and in terms of conflicts of personal integrity. To this end, we argue, an agent can be wronged by way of the added exposure to moral risk entailed by moral exploitation. Furthermore, as we have alluded to in Chapters 1 and 2, by overexposing vulnerable parties to situations where the incurring of moral residue is highly likely or inevitable, we also wrong such persons in this unique and additional way even in cases where no moral residue was incurred.

3. The Moral Exploitation of Soldiers

Criticism E: "You shouldn't have joined then!"

Response E:
By now we hope we have made the case that there are good reasons to think this objection is not so simple. Given the epistemic vulnerabilities of recruits due to age, as well as other noted vulnerabilities related to socioeconomics, demographics, region, and so forth, combined with the slick and often misleading recruitment content and incentivization, we believe a recruit's ostensibly free choice to not join up is, upon further inspection, not so free. What's more, and this is the crucial point, we are not analyzing possible manipulative or exploitative relationships existing between customers or workers with respect to some free-market entity. Rather, we are analyzing the exploitative relationship existing between *the state and its citizenry* and the state's explicit appeal to *duty* as part of its set of recruitment appeals. Given this explicit appeal to duty, the retort of caveat emptor, or "buyer beware," is categorically inapt. Indeed, in a social order with a more just distribution of moral responsibilities amongst the demos, this otherwise noble and natural instinct to want to fulfill that duty to serve and to protect one's homeland would make sense and would not therefore require such slick and sophisticated recruitment methods.

Criticism F: "You're infantilizing soldiers! Soldiers aren't victims!"

Response F:

Once again, our claim here isn't that young recruits are wholly incapable of making adult decisions for themselves. Our claim is that with respect to *the moral realities of present-day warfighting specifically*, age and its concomitant cognitive and epistemic constraints make it the case that young recruits are vulnerable to wrongful exploitation in certain respects. As we have noted, society regards age to be morally relevant in other domains like voting, marriage, sex, driving, alcohol consumption, and so on. Killing and breaking stuff on behalf of the demos, we argue, is yet another domain where age is morally relevant.

With respect to the specific charge that "soldiers aren't victims," we wholeheartedly agree. They certainly aren't. However, we believe that there is a substantive difference between whining and playing the victim versus having a basic notion of recognition respect and a duty of self-regard. We believe that soldiers' and veterans' oath to the Constitution does not thereby equate to carte blanche subordination, self-abnegation, and martyrdom on behalf of the collective will of a radically apathetic civilian demos in perpetuity.

Question G: What's wrong with letting a young person serve their country?

Response G:

On its face, this seems like a simple enough question/objection. However, we believe that this question is much more complex than it appears, as is our response. First, let us be clear that we do not believe that it is wrong to allow young citizens to fulfill their desire to serve their country. As we will argue in Chapter 5, we believe that there is in fact a strong prima facie duty of citizenship that all citizens, young and old alike, serve their country in *some* capacity. Our main issue, and indeed the main motivation for writing this book, is the radically uneven distribution of warfighting responsibilities that have ended up on the shoulders of an increasingly thin sliver of society who is often vulnerable in certain epistemic regards due to age. This is why in Chapter 5, we argued for the moral requirement to return to a draft or mandatory national service model. In this regard, we can make a distinction between young persons serving in a nonmilitary national service capacity (in forestry, nature and infrastructure building, or humanitarian aid), in an exclusively homeland defense capacity (like the Swiss model), and/or in a front-facing expeditionary capacity. With respect to this expeditionary capacity, we believe that age-related epistemic constraints should then factor much more heavily into recruitment targeting, selection, and screening.

Criticism H: If we raise the age of military recruitment to an ostensibly non-exploitative age range, then what is society going to do with a surplus of restless, fighting-aged men?

Response H:

This is a perennial pragmatic problem that all civil societies have had to deal with. This pragmatic issue also has tremendous moral import and therefore weighs heavily on the moral scales. It might just turn out that all things considered, despite the moral exploitation of soldiers, some combination of moral and prudential reasons ultimately speaks to keeping the recruitment age, pitch, and structure fundamentally the same. We believe, however, that there are other institutional solutions that can at once solve the moral exploitation of soldiers and this problem of the surplus of fighting-aged young men. As we noted, and as articulated in Chapter 5, we believe a draft or mandatory national service model (to include nonmilitary service) could split this difference.

Criticism I: If it is an all-things-considered good to have a standing, professional military to defend a free and just society, then it might just be a necessary evil to exploit or mislead a certain portion of society in order to fill the military's ranks. Put another way, were America to be fully honest and non-exploitative in its recruitment content, recruitment practices, and demographic targeting, then it would pragmatically impossible for the American military to fill its ranks.[3]

Response I:

With respect to the first part of this argument, it very well might be the case that it is a necessary evil to have some form of a military in order that free and just societies be protected. However, firstly, the growing preponderance of evidence that has been steadily accumulating for the last half century, at least with respect to the American project, suggests that such a model might not be the most ethical or *even prudent* way for America to continue to defend itself. Such evidence includes the moral hazard of professional militaries being used in an increasing number of expeditionary and adventurist projects, the increased institutional incentivization for wars to continue without foreseeable end, an increased disconnect between the military body and the civilian principle who controls it as well as civilian society and its returning veterans, the civilian principle not having any "skin in the game" physically or psychologically speaking or in terms of a felt sense of moral responsibility, as well as a

---

[3] Seth Lazar, "The Moral Responsibility of Volunteer Soldiers," *Boston Review,* November 6, 2013, https://bostonreview.net/forum/moral-wounds/seth-lazar-moral-wounds-lazar.

host of second-order side effects such as increased numbers of veteran suicide, PTSD, and moral injury, homeless, divorce, and so forth.

Second, even if it was the case that an all-volunteer force was the best way for America to continue to defend itself and its interests, it is not at all obvious or certain that exploiting and misleading young recruits would be *the only* way America could field its forces effectively. Indeed, one criticism of America's failure in Vietnam was because of MacNamara's decision to use low-IQ soldiers. A similar argument could be made with respect to the folly of using young soldiers that lack both the mental hardware and epistemic software to fully grasp the moral weight of the fight that they might be taking part in. By setting up such a situation whereby young soldiers are exploitatively recruited, not only are we increasing the chances that such soldiers might make moral and prudential mistakes on the battlefield, but we are also increasing the chances that we will be reaping those hastily sewn seeds on the back end of the military service transaction in the form of a subclass of morally traumatized, listless veterans within society. Hence, a higher recruitment age and an honest recruitment pitch about the moral content of war might not only function as a more moral and non-exploitative means of defending America but also might mitigate a dearth of increasing social ills back home. As we note, this is but one option for institutional reform however.

Criticism J: Soldiers have been compensated adequately. Consequently, civilian society does not owe them anything further after their service obligation. In other words, "a deal's a deal."

Response J:
One immediate reply can be made here that borrows from Wertheimer's point about exploited college athletes. One of the main points Wertheimer drives home about college athletes is that they are often recruited under the misleading narrative that they will be able to trade their athletic labor to a college or university in exchange for a decent if not exceptional university education. Wertheimer, however, points out that what is often not emphasized for these students is that they will be practicing so often and will be so physically exhausted from frequent games and practices that the realistic chances of uptake, absorption, and assimilation of that top-tier higher education oftentimes does not have any sufficient opportunity to go through. A similar argument can be made with respect to the absence of sufficient uptake conditions for many American recruits who opt into the military on the assumption that they will receive "educational knowledge" and "translatable job skills" for the civilian world after their time in service. Accordingly, the common notion that soldiers who have served have been adequately compensated is false. This is so since there is strong empirical evidence suggesting that many soldiers are so institutionalized from military service that the compensatory benefits

they ostensibly should have received fail to meet the uptake conditions promised or suggested at the original time of contract. Bracketing such arguments about uptake conditions for compensation, the main point of our account has been that *moral responsibility* for warfighting has been disproportionately outsourced and piled upon a small set of vulnerable persons in society by the rest of society via our present institutional arrangements. We have likewise argued that, in so doing, those within society who did not take on this particular responsibility of military service nonetheless engendered a *new* set of duties of their own to conscientiously, wisely, and ethically direct the initiation, conduct, and stewardship of such wars and warfighters those volunteers agreed to. We have given both historical and current events as evidence to suggest that, to quote Andrew Bacevich, a "breach of trust" has occurred between the military and the civilian principle and civilian society at large, which has shirked its civic duties and failed to uphold its end of the bargain. If this is the case, then compensation to soldiers in the form of money, medical benefits, education, governmental jobs, and so forth, *even if sufficient uptake conditions are met*, is simply the wrong *kind* of thing or category for which to compensate the shouldering of such excess moral responsibility. To cite Walzer once again, what we seem to have here is a "blocked exchange" and a fundamental *incommensurability* between certain goods for certain services. We might think of the moral exploitation of soldiers then as a particularly severe or pronounced instance of a blocked exchanges case. We might also think that if soldiers have come to take on moral residue, or dirty hands, on behalf of the greater civilian society, then the redistribution of goods and services is simply inapt in its capacity to morally resolve such moral residue.[4]

Criticism K: More ex post compensation for past exploited soldiers actually sets up a situation of pernicious inducement, whereby back-end compensation in the form of medical or educational benefits ironically creates unintended conditions of incentivization for future young recruits.

Response K:

This argument or versions of this argument derive primarily from Jennifer Middlestadt's *The Rise of the Military Welfare State.*[5] The worry here can be expressed more precisely as follows. If we recognize that past/previous soldiers have been exploited (standardly and/or morally) and society aims to remedy this unfair distribution by giving such persons more robust

---

[4] For a more thorough articulation of this objection and a philosophical response to it, see Steve Kershnar, *Gratitude toward Veterans: Why Americans Should Not Be Very Grateful to Veterans* (London, 2014) and Michael Robillard, "A Case for Gratitude: A Response to Steve Kershnar's Gratitude towards Veterans," *Reason Papers*, 39, no. 1 (2017): 65–73.

[5] See J. Middlestadt, *Rise of the Military Welfare State* (Cambridge, MA: 2018).

compensation ex post in the form of more medical incentives, more government job opportunities, and more college educational benefits, then, in so doing, such a robust set of incentives offered on the back end of military service would likely serve to further incentivize and attract the next young generation of potential recruits on the front end. Join the military and "you'll be set for life" so the thought might go. Accordingly, the danger here is that by attempting to compensate one set of token exploited persons, such compensation actually foreseeably functions as a stronger set of incentives that facilitate the exploitation of future type persons over a longer iterative game.

We agree with Middlestadt that this danger of pernicious inducement is a weighty and serious consideration to worry about with respect to giving veteran compensation in the form of more medical or education or job opportunities. One thought, however, might be that increasing veteran compensation on the back end is only permissible on the condition that adequate front-end changes are made beforehand. Hence, the thought here is that adequate compensation could still be given ex post to prior exploited veterans without it facilitating pernicious inducement since the content of the recruitment pitch would be more accurate and representative of the responsibilities of warfighting as well as the age of recruitment increased to prevent such incentivization entering the choice world of such young persons at all. This is one way in which Middlestadt's worry could be curtailed. The other more sweeping solution that could help abate Middlestadt's worries is to simply switch to a draft or mandatory service model.

Criticism L: The redistributing of associative duties within society is pragmatically impossible.

Another objection to the concept of moral exploitation is derived from an argument by Bob Goodin. Let us call this *Goodin's Challenge.*[6] In, "What Is So Special about Our Fellow Countrymen?," Goodin points out that while we may all have a general duty of rescue, the discharging of this duty by all parties, all at the same time, would likely result in a far worse state of affairs than were no one to act at all.[7] Imagine, for instance, a person drowning in the ocean, and every person on the beach, all at once, attempting to save that individual. In such a scenario, not only would such an attempt be highly inefficient in bringing about the intended result, in all likelihood it would also create greater risk of drowning for all of rescuers involved. Hence, despite all agents having this positive duty of rescue, pragmatism demands that some persons (i.e., lifeguards) be assigned as the official agents who have the special associative

---

[6] This portion borrowed directly from our "On the Moral Exploitation of Soldiers" article.

[7] Robert Goodin, "What is So Special about Our Fellow Countrymen?" *Ethics* 98, no. 4 (July 1988): 663–86.

duty to perform the rescue on behalf of the rest of the community while everyone else refrains from acting.

One implication of Goodin's Challenge then is the notion that, pragmatically speaking, it seems fundamentally infeasible for us to distribute associative duties equally across all members of a society or even within a small group of persons. The brute facts of life, pragmatics, and efficiency will likely demand that some minority of agents bear the burden of discharging certain associative duties, within certain contexts, on behalf of the greater community while other agents refrain from carrying out such duties. Accordingly, it is not then as if soldiers, doctors, nurses, police officers, firefighters, and so forth are being morally exploited by society in virtue of the added responsibilities that accompany their special roles, rather, it is just an undeniable fact that someone will have to serve in these roles regardless, and not everyone can do so all at once. The fact that society does not distribute these associative duties among all members equally is therefore not indicative of unfairness or of exploitation, since the redistribution of duties in such a manner would be pragmatically impossible. Assuming one accepts that "ought implies can," a proponent of Goodin's Challenge would conclude that the pragmatic impossibility of are distribution of associative duties amongst all agents in society entails that there is in fact, no corresponding duty to do so.

Response L:

The fundamental problem with this objection is that it makes the inference from the pragmatic need within society to have an unequal distribution of associative duties in some contexts and roles to the conclusion that the way by which those roles are filled cannot be of a more or less equitable form. Consider, for instance, a tribal scenario where it makes pragmatic sense for us to only have one leader during our hunts. While it makes sense to have only one leader during the hunts and to not have twenty leaders for instance, we would likely think it unfair if the tribe demanded that the same person lead the hunts every time, without being allowed to trade out occasionally with other equally capable members. Thus, even though the pragmatics of hunting dictate that the most efficient way for us to achieve our ends is to have one leader, it does not follow that we must saddle the same individual, time and time again, with the weighty responsibility of keeping the entire tribe alive by his own wits when other equally capable persons could assume that role at times. In this same way, one can be morally exploited when the distribution of morally weighty group roles falls frequently and unequitably upon the shoulders of vulnerable agents. Or, as we have suggested, were the same leader to stay in place however, then there should arguably be some corresponding and proportionate ex post compensation after the hunts in terms of additional decision-making power and capacity within the demos.

Criticism M: Aren't young recruits only responsible for their particular roles in combat? Hence, won't mid-tier and senior-level military leadership be the proper locus for moral responsibility?

Response M:

This is generally a correct point about apportioning in bello responsibilities in combat. However, it is important to note that fully made senior leadership does not drop out of the ether ex nihilo. Rather, recruits who eventually become senior leaders likely also entered the recruitment funnel at a very young age. So our general point about the exploitative recruitment structure still holds true.

While this set of replies is far from exhaustive, we at least feel we have given here our best attempt at answering some of the major questions and objections regarding the internal conceptual tensions of our argument, several adjacent and background concepts connected to our view, and have addressed some important related contingent concerns.

Bibliography

Aamodt, Sandra, "Brain Maturity Extends Well beyond Teen Years." *NPR*, October 10, 2011.

Alexandra, Andrew, Dean-Peter Baker, Marina Caparini, eds., *Private Military and Security Companies: Ethics, Policies, and Civil-Military Relations*. London: Routledge, 2008.

Allen, Charles, "Skin in the Game: Poor Kids and Patriots/Breach of Trust: How Americans Failed Their Soldiers and Their Country." *Parameters*, 44 (2014), 114–16.

"America's Army" Blurs Virtual War, "Militainment." *Morning Edition from NPR*, March 2, 2020.

Arplay, Nomy, "On Acting Rationally against One's Best Judgement." *Ethics*, 110 (2000), 488–513.

Asoni, Andrea, et al., "A Mercenary Army of the Poor? Technological Change and the Demographic Composition of the Post-9/11 U.S. Military." *Journal of Strategic Studies*, 43, no. 1 (2020), 1–47.

Bacevich, Andrew, *Breach of Trust: How Americans Failed Their Soldiers and Their Country*. New York, 2013.

Bazargan, Saba, "Moral Coercion." *Philosopher.s Imprint*, 14 (2014), 1–18.

Berkhout, Suze G., "Buns in the Oven: Objectification, Surrogacy, and Women's Autonomy." *Social Theory and Practice*, 34, no. 1 (2008), 95–117.

Bender, James, et al., "Some States Have Much Higher Enlistment Rates Than Others." *Business Insider*, July 20, 2014.

Brooks, Rosa, "How the Pentagon Became Walmart." *FP*, August 9, 2016.

Camlot, Jason, "Alfred Lord Tennyson, 'The Charge of the Light Brigade' (1854)." *Victorian Review*, 35 (2009), 7–32.

"Congress Questions Whether U.S. Special Operations Forces Should Remain in High Demand." *All Things Considered from NPR*, May 7, 2019.

"Demographics of the U.S. Military." Council on Foreign Relations, July 13, 2020.

Desch, Michael C., "America's (Dis) Regard for Its Soldiers and Veterans." *The American Conservative*, August 1, 2017.

Ellner, Andrea, et al., *When Soldiers Say No: Selective Conscientious Objection in the Modern Military*. Burlington, VT, 2014.

Feinberg, Joel, "Noncoercive Exploitation." In *Paternalism*, edited by Rolf Satorius, 201–235. Minneapolis, 1983.

Feinberg, Joel, *Rights, Justice, and the Bounds of Liberty*. Princeton, NJ, 1980.

Fountain, Ben, *Billy Lynn's Long Halftime Walk*. New York, 2012.

Fox, Justin, "Why You Don't Know Anybody in the Military." *Bloomberg*, October 20, 2017.

Goodin, Robert, *Exploiting a Situation and Exploiting a Person*. University of Essex, 1985.

Goodin, Robert, "What Is So Special about Our Fellow Countrymen?" *Ethics*, 98 (1998), 663–686.

Hardy, Thomas, "The Man He Killed." *The British Journal of Psychiatry*, 205 (2014), 274.

Harman, Elizabeth, "Does Moral Ignorance Exculpate?" *Ratio Special Issue: Developing Deontology*, 24 (2011), 443–468.

Jenkins, Ryan, Robillard, Michael, Strawser, Bradley, eds. *Who Should Die?: The Ethics of Killing in War*. Oxford, 2017.

Johnson, W. J., *Bhagavad Gita*. Oxford, 2008.

Johnston, Windsor, "War Games Lure Recruits for 'Real Thing." *NPR* , July 31, 2010.

Junger, Sebastian, "How PTSD Became a Problem Far beyond the Battlefield." *Vanity Fair*, May 7, 2015.

Junger, Sebastian, *Tribe: On Homecoming and Belonging*. New York, 2016.

Junger, Sebastian, "Sebastian Junger: U.S. Veterans Need to Share the Moral Burden of War." *Washington Post*, May 24, 2013.

Kanarakis, Evan, "For God, Country, and Profit?" *The Cud*, 2005.

Kane, Tim, "Who Bears the Burden? Demographic Characteristics of U.S. Military Recruits before and after 9/11." Heritage Foundation, November 7, 2005.

Kershnar, Steve, *Gratitude toward Veterans: Why Americans Should Not Be Very Grateful to Veterans*. Washington, DC, 2014.

Kipling, Rudyard, *Barrack Room Ballads*. New York, 1900.

Lazar, Seth, "The Moral Responsibility of Volunteer Soldiers." *Boston Review*, November 6, 2013.

Lazar, Seth. "The Responsibility Dilemma for Killing in War: A Review Essay." *Philosophy & Public Affairs*, 38 (2010), 180–213.

Liberto, Hallie, "Exploitation and the Vulnerability Clause." *Ethical Theory and Moral Practice*, 17 (2014), 619–29.

Liberto, Hallie, "Noxious Markets versus Noxious Gift Relationships." *Social Theory and Practice*, 39 (2013), 265–287.

Limkin, Alex E., "Letter to a Dead Colonel." *Alibi*, March 20, 2008.

Lucas, George, "This Is Not Your Father's War—Confronting the Moral Challenges of 'Unconventional' War." *Journal of National Security Law & Policy* 3, no. 2 (2009), 329–340.

MacIntyre, Alasdair, *Is Patriotism a Virtue?* Lawrence, 2002.

McCarthy, Shane, "Would Lowering the Age of Recruitment Fix the Military's Recruiting Worries?" *Military Times*, July 10, 2019.

McMahan, Jeff, "Revising the Doctrine of Double Effect." *Journal of Applied Philosophy*, 11 (1994), 201–212.

McMahan, Jeff, *Killing in War*. Oxford, 2009.

Meyers, Chris, "Wrongful Beneficence: Exploitation and Third World Sweatshops." *Journal of Social Philosophy* 35 (2004), 319–333.

Oberdiek, John, "Lost in Moral Space: On the Infringing/Violating Distinction and Its Place in the Theory of Rights." *Law and Philosophy*, 23 (2004), 325–346.

Office of the Under Secretary of Defense for Personnel and Readiness, "Applicants for Active Component Enlistment, FY11: by Service, Gender, and Age with Civilian Comparison Group." 2016.

Office of the Under Secretary of Defense for Personnel and Readiness, "Manpower and Reserve Affairs." 2013.

Office of the Under Secretary of Defense for Personnel and Readiness, "Population Representation in the Military Services: Fiscal Year 2016 Summary Report." 2016.

Orwell, George, *1984*. San Diego, 1984.

Parry, Jonathan, "Defensive Harm, Consent, and Intervention." *Philosophy and Public Affairs*, 45 (2017), 356–396.

Pew Research Center. "War and Sacrifice in the Post-9/11 Era." 2011.

Philipps, Dave, and Tim Arango, "Who Signs Up to Fight: Make Up of U.S. Recruits Shows Glaring Disparity." *New York Times*, January 10, 2020.

Press, Eyal, "The Wounds of the Drone Warrior." *New York Times*, June 13, 2018.

Rangel, Charles B., "The US Military Is as Unequal as America: Want a Fair Fight? Reinstate the Draft." *Guardian*, September 30, 2014.

Robillard, Michael, and Strawser, Bradley, "Are Soldiers Morally Exploited?" *Stockholm Center for War and Peace Blog*, 2016.

Robillard, Michael, and Strawser, Bradley, "The Moral Exploitation of Soldiers." *Public Affairs Quarterly*, 30 (2016): 171–196.

Rodin, David, *War and Self-Defense*. Oxford, 2002.

Rogin, Josh, "McChrystal: Time to Bring Back the Draft." *FP*, July 3, 2012.

Rosen, Gideon, "Culpability and Ignorance." *Proceedings of the Aristotelian Society*, 103 (2003), 61–84.

Ryan, Cheyney, *The Chickenhawk Syndrome: War, Sacrifice, and Personal Responsibility*. Lanham, MD, 2009.

Sample, Ruth, *Exploitation: What It Is and Why It's Wrong*. Lanham, MD, 2003.

Satz, Debra, *Why Some Things Should Not Be for Sale: The Moral Limits of Markets*. New York, 2010.

Satz, Debra, "Markets in Women's Sexual Labor." *Ethics*, 106 (1995), 63–85.

Sats, Debra, and Zwolinski, Matt, *Where Are the Moral Limits of Markets?* McGill University, 2013.

Schacherer, Rachel-Ann. "Conditions Affecting Military Enlistments." *The Public Purpose* Vol. III (2005): 76–82.

Schafer, Amy, "The Warrior Caste: America Increasingly Relies on a Small Group of Multi-Generational Military Families to Fight Its Wars. That's a Problem." *Slate*, August 2, 2017.

Scharre, Paul, *Army of None: Autonomous Weapons and the Future of War*. New York, 2019.

Seck, Hope Hodge, "Sebastian Junger's Draft Proposal: Service with Non-Military Options." Military.com, July 18, 2016.

Sen, Amartya, *Development as Freedom*. Oxford, 1999.

Sen, Amartya, *Resources, Values, and Development*. Oxford, 1984.

Sherman, Nancy, *Afterwar: Healing the Moral Injuries of Our Soldiers*. New York, 2015.

Sherman, Nancy, *The Untold War: Inside the Hearts, Minds, and Souls of Our Soldiers*. New York, 2011.

Shiffrin, Seana Valentine, "Paternalism, Unconscionability Doctrine, and Accommodation." *Philosophy and Public Affairs*, 29 (2000), 205–251.

Steinhoff, Uwe, "Yet Another Revised DDE? A Note on David K. Chan's DDEd." *Ethical Theory and Moral Practice*, 9 (2006), 231–236.

Strawser, Bradley Jay, "Revisionist Just War Theory and the Real World: A Cautiously Optimistic Proposal." In *Routledge Handbook of Ethics and War: Just War Theory in the 21st Century*, edited by Fritz Allhoff, Adan Henschke, and Nick Evans, 76–89. London, 2013.

Strawser, Bradley Jay, "Walking the Tightrope of Just War." *Analysis*, 71 (2011), 533–544.

Tennyson, Alfred Lord, "The Charge of the Light Brigade." *The Charge of the Light Brigade and Other Poems*. Mineola, NY, 1992.

Thomson, Judith Jarvis, *The Realm of Rights*. Cambridge, MA, 1990.

Thomson, Judith Jarvis. *Rights, Restitution and Risk*. (London, 1986).

US Department of Defense, "2015 Demographics Report." 2015.

Valdman, Mikhail, "A Theory of Wrongful Exploitation." *Philosophers Imprint*, 9 (2009), 1–14.

Valdman, Mikhail, "Exploitation and Injustice." *Social Theory and Practice*, 34, no. 4 (2008), 551–572.

Vogel, Stephen, "White House Proposes Cuts in Military Recruiting Budget." *Washington Post*, May 11, 2009.

Walzer, Michael, *Just and Unjust Wars: A Moral Argument with Historical Illustrations*. New York, 2000.

Watkins, Shanea, and Sherk, James, "Who Serves in the U.S. Military? The Demographics of Enlisted Troops and Officers." The Heritage Foundation, August 21, 2008.

Wertheimer, Alan, *Exploitation*. Princeton, NJ, 1996.

Wertheimer, Alan, "Two Questions about Commercial Surrogacy." *Philosophy & Public Affairs*, 21 (1992), 211–239.

Woodside, Stephen J. "Who Should Die?: The Ethics of Killing in War." Review of *Who Should Die? The Ethics of Killing in War,* by Ryan Jenkins, Michael Robillard, and Bradley J. Strawser. *Notre Dame Philosophical Reviews* (2018).

Williams, Bernard, "Critique of Utilitarianism." In *Utilitarianism: For and against,* edited by JJC Smart and Bernard Williams, 77–135. Cambridge, UK, 1973.

Wood, Allen W. "Exploitation." *Social Philosophy and Policy,* 12, no. 2 (1995), 136–158.

Zwolinski, Matt, "Structural Exploitation." *Social Philosophy and Policy,* 29, no. 1 (2012), 154–179.

Zwolinski, Matt. "Sweatshops, Choice, and Exploitation." *Philosophy: Faculty Scholarship,* 17 (2007): 689–727.

Index

For the benefit of digital users, indexed terms that span two pages (e.g., 52–53) may, on occasion, appear on only one of those pages.

Figures are indicated by *f* following the page number